# Time for HOMEWORK

Colleen
Timoshenko

# 3

## Book 3

Hunter Education Nightingale

HUNTER EDUCATION NIGHTINGALE


Time for Homework - Book 3

Published by:
Hunter Education Nightingale
ABN: 69 055 798 626
PO Box 547
Warners Bay NSW 2282
Ph: 0417 658 777
email: sales@huntereducationnightingale.com.au
paul@huntereducationnightingale.com.au
www.huntereducationnightingale.com.au

Cover Design: Doriana Berkovic

National Library of Australia Card No.
and ISBN 978 - 1 - 922242 - 27 - 3



F E D C B A
19 18 17 16 15 14

# Time for Homework

## *Book 3*

## About this Book

*Time for Homework Book 3* is the fourth in a series of seven books written to help reinforce many of the concepts, skills and understanding needed for today's school curriculum.

The series is designed as a user friendly resource to improve a student's reading skills, knowledge of grammar, accuracy in spelling and improved word knowledge through word building activities. Questions covering the New Mathematics Curriculum complete each unit.

The book contains 30 units of work and one unit can be attempted each week. Each unit addresses the subjects outlined above and covers topics in today's environment which are relevant to the new Australian Curriculum for English and Mathematics.

As the child gains a better knowledge of language; reading, interpreting and responding to the written text develops and improves. Knowledge of grammar, punctuation and spelling, as well as mathematics is acquired by completing the set activities.

While *Time for Homework* treats many of the topics presented in the school curriculum, it is a summary only of those subjects. This book is fun to use at home, with the child, as a resource, to develop and improve learning.

## Message to Parents

*With Time for Homework, Book 3*, your child should not need help with reading or the explanation of instructions. As a parent you are asked to support your child's learning but resist the temptation to provide answers. By all means, read a word for your child if necessary and then support him/her to gain a better knowledge about the word and its meaning. This reassures the child and enables one to become a more independent learner. As the child works through the book your encouragement may be all that is needed.

Regular homework helps your child develop skills which will assist in the learning process and improve confidence over time. A confident and skilled learner will enjoy school.

Praise your child at all times because you are the ideal support person in your child's life. Use this book together to make the learning process more meaningful for both of you.

*Time for Homework, Book 3* is designed as a fun book for home use. Enjoy the journey!

## Our Annual Camping Holiday

We were packed and ready to leave. Mum was in the front, sitting beside dad who was driving. Josie and I had been woken from a deep sleep, just so we could be on the road before the traffic built up.

Of course, we were grumpy and still too tired to take any notice of the two adults packing the car for our annual camping trip up north. We knew though that we would have plenty of time to catch up on some sleep during the trip.

Because we were so sleepy, when dad pulled away from the garage, in the early morning light, we didn't see anything missing. It wasn't until our first stop, two hours later, when mum noticed it! The tents were not on top of the car. They were nowhere to be found.

Now what was dad going to do?

### Understanding

Use the narrative to answer each question.

a. Why were the children woken early? ____________________

b. Where were they sitting? ____________________

c. How often did the family go camping? ____________________

d. What was missing for the camping trip? ____________________

e. How far into the journey were they before the mistake was found?

____________________

### Interpreting

Circle T (true) or F (false) to answer correctly.

| | | |
|---|---|---|
| a. Dad was in the front and mum was driving. | T | F |
| b. There are 4 children in the car. | T | F |
| c. I have a sister. | T | F |
| d. We were happy to be woken for the trip. | T | F |
| e. It took a long time to reach the camp. | T | F |

### Language: Noun Groups

1. Underline all the noun groups in the following sentence:

Josie and I had cornflakes and toast before we left home.

2. How would you help dad solve the problem? (Resolution)

____________________

____________________

____________________

## Spelling

Look, cover, write, check each word.

were ______________ ☐

was ______________ ☐

pack ______________ ☐

woke ______________ ☐

garage ______________ ☐

notice ______________ ☐

found ______________ ☐

grumpy ______________ ☐

annual ______________ ☐

north ______________ ☐

## Word Building

Add '**ed**' to these words.

pack ______________

pull ______________

found ______________

These words need the last letter doubled to add '**ed**'.

slap ______________

rob ______________

skip ______________

stop ______________

pat ______________

## Sentences: Nouns name people, places and things

Fill in the blanks using a suitable noun from these words.

**WORD BANK:** mum Josie garage dad tents

a. The ______________ were nowhere to be found!

b. My sister, ______________ and I were too sleepy to care.

c. It was ______________ who saw the ______________ were missing.

d. What do you think ______________ thought when he found out?

## The Centimetre

1. How many centimetres in length are these?

a. 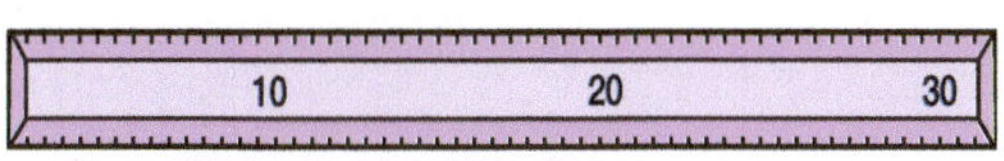

☐

b. 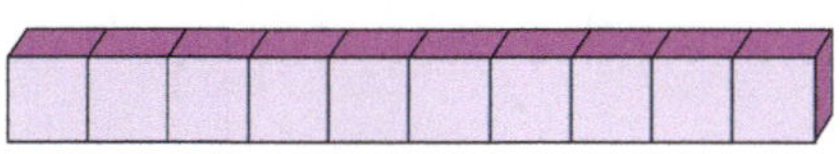
☐

c. 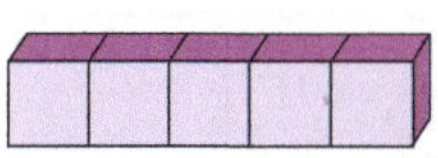
☐

2. Measure the width of this book.

☐ cm

## Time

1. Match the digital time to its analogue time.

a. 

e. 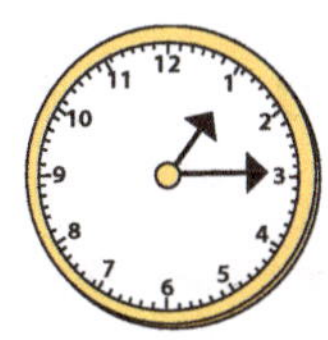

b. 

f. 

c. 

g. 

d. 

h. 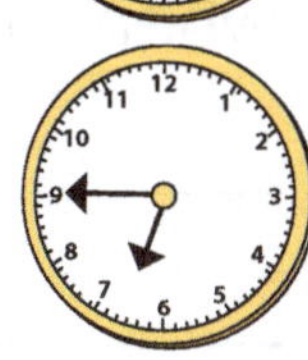

The Internet is the term used to describe the millions of sites and pages which are connected by links around the world. There are many ways to use the Internet.

**www:** The World Wide Web, or as it is commonly called the Internet, connects millions of people across the globe. It makes using this tool easy for people. Without access to the Web you cannot search for information easily.

**Search Engines:** These make it possible for information to be sifted and sorted very quickly. When key words are entered into a search engine it crawls the web, to find and locate information that is available on the topic.

**Email:** This is used for sending and receiving electronic mail to and from personal computers and business networks to help speed up communication with friends and industry.

## Understanding

Tick the box if you can find this information in the text.

- **a.** Millions of people can connect to each other through the Internet. ☐
- **b.** The Internet is commonly called The Web. ☐
- **c.** It is easy to find information on the Web. ☐
- **d.** Electronic mail is used by individuals and companies for its convenience. ☐
- **e.** Snail mail is very seldom used now. ☐

## Interpreting

Use a word from the Word Bank to complete each sentence.

**WORD BANK:** Email Search Engine World Wide Web The Internet

- **a.** To find information for my project I can use ______________________.
- **b.** It is quick and easy to find information using a ______________________.
- **c.** I can send my friend a letter using ______________________.
- **d.** Another name for the Internet is ______________________.

## Language

Adjectives describe nouns. Chose an adjective from the story for each noun.

**1. a.** ______________ words **b.** ______________ engines

**c.** ______________ mail **d.** ______________ networks

**e.** ______________ computers **f.** ______________ mail

Write this sentence using full stops and capital letters correctly where needed.

**2.** when i use the internet i need to spell correctly if i want to find information

______________________________________________

______________________________________________

## Spelling

Look, cover, write, check each word.

term ____________ ☐

used ____________ ☐

links ____________ ☐

World ____________ ☐

common ____________ ☐

business ____________ ☐

locate ____________ ☐

possible ____________ ☐

## Word Building

**The rule is:** 'i' comes before '**e**' except after '**c**'. Circle and then write the correct word.

| | | |
|---|---|---|
| piece | peice | ____________ |
| neice | niece | ____________ |
| chief | cheif | ____________ |
| theif | thief | ____________ |
| believe | beleive | ____________ |
| breif | brief | ____________ |

Circle the incorrect words in this sentence:

Mary saw going to het ship four sum milk.

## Sentences: Statements tell us facts.

Match each sentence beginning to its correct ending.

- **a.** The World Wide Web
- **c.** Key words are important
- **e.** Access to the Web is needed
- **g.** A search engine
- **i.** Electronic mail can be sent

- **b.** is used to sift and sort information.
- **d.** to and from personal computers.
- **f.** when using search engines.
- **h.** is another name for the Internet.
- **j.** for information to be found.

## Place Value

**1.** Write the number shown on each place value card.

**a.**

| TH | H | T | O |
|---|---|---|---|
| \|\|\| | \|\|\|\| | \|\| | \|\|\|\|\|\| |

____________

**b.**

| TH | H | T | O |
|---|---|---|---|
| \| | \|\|\| | \|\|\|\|\|\|\| | \|\|\|\|\|\| |

____________

**2.** Write the place value as thousands, hundreds, tens or ones for each circled number.

**a.** 7 2 4 (3) ____________

**b.** 8 (6) 1 4 ____________

## Number Facts

Fill in missing number facts in each group.

**1. a.** 5 + 0 = [5]  **2. a.** 5 - 0 = [ ]

**b.** 4 + 1 = [ ]  **b.** 5 - 4 = [ ]

**c.** 3 + 2 = [ ]  **c.** 5 - [ ] = 2

**2.** Look for combinations of 10 to help with addition. One is done for you.

8 + 7 + 2 = 10 + 7

**a.** 6+5+4=[ ]  **b.** 8+7+3=[ ]

**c.** 5+4+5=[ ]  **d.** 1+6+9=[ ]

**e.** 3+2+8=[ ]  **f.** 5+4+6=[ ]

In 1952, the then 26 year old Princess Elizabeth and her husband, the Duke of Edinburgh, were on holiday in Kenya.

While they were there the King of England died. Because he was Princess Elizabeth's father and the princess was heir to the throne she now became Queen Elizabeth. She and the duke had to return to England immediately. This was a very sad time for everyone in the Royal Family.

Sometime after her return, preparations were made for the queen's coronation. The young queen's coronation was held in Westminster Abbey on 2 June,1953. It was the same abbey that she and her husband had been married in six years earlier. Then her only two children, Prince Charles and Princess Anne, attended the ceremony. They were five and three years old. It was a big occasion and all of England and The Commonwealth celebrated.

In 2012 the queen celebrated 60 years on the throne.

## Understanding

Shade the bubble to best answers each question.

**a.** Why did Princess Elizabeth go to Kenya?

- ◯ she went to see the tigers
- ◯ it was hunting season
- ◯ for a holiday
- ◯ to visit friends

**b.** Who was 'heir' to the throne?

- ◯ Princess Anne
- ◯ The Duke of Edinburgh
- ◯ Princess Elizabeth
- ◯ Prince Charles

**c.** Who was with her in Kenya?

- ◯ her two children
- ◯ her husband
- ◯ the king
- ◯ her friends

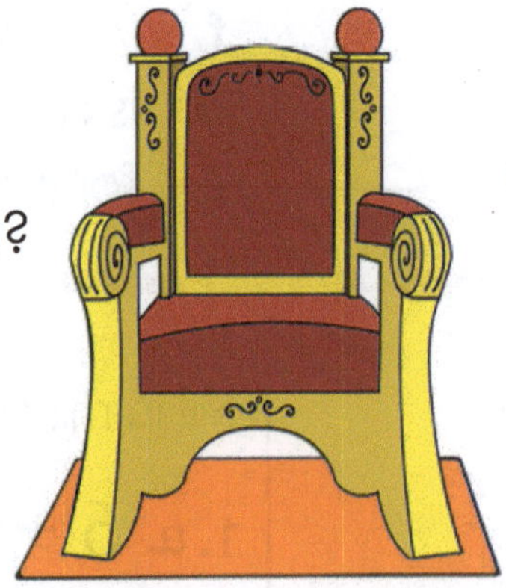

**d.** How many children went with the Princess to Kenya?

- ◯ one
- ◯ two
- ◯ three
- ◯ none

## Interpreting

Write your answer to the following questions.

**a.** How long before the new queen was crowned?____________________

**b.** Where did the coronation take place?____________________

**c.** How old was the queen in 2012?____________________

**d.** How old is Prince Charles and Princess Anne now?____________________

## Language

Underline the **verbs in the past tense** in each sentence.

**a.** The royal couple were on holiday in Kenya.
**b.** The king was Princess Elizabeth's father.
**c.** Charles and Anne attended the ceremony.
**d.** All of England and the Commonwealth celebrated.

## Spelling

Look, cover, write, check each word.

prince ________ ☐
duke ________ ☐
princess ________ ☐
king ________ ☐
queen ________ ☐
earl ________ ☐
viscount ________ ☐
duchess ________ ☐
lord ________ ☐
lady ________ ☐

## Word Building

Add 'ing' to the following words.
**Rule:** Double the last letter

sit ________
rub ________
jet ________
step ________
skip ________
drop ________
chop ________
slap ________

## Sentences

Write the subject and the verb in each sentence in the correct column.

***Subject:*** Person spoken about.
***Verb:*** action, feeling, thinking or helping word.

| | SUBJECT | VERB |
|---|---|---|
| **a.** The princess was in Kenya. | ________ | ________ |
| **b.** The king died in 1952. | ________ | ________ |
| **c.** We celebrated together. | ________ | ________ |
| **d.** I thought for a long time. | ________ | ________ |

## Money

Tick the coins needed to buy each item.

**a.**

**b.**

## Chance

Roll a dice ten times. Write the turned up face for each throw.

☐ ☐ ☐ ☐ ☐

☐ ☐ ☐ ☐ ☐

**a.** Which number turned up **most**? ☐

**b.** Which number turned up **least**? ☐

**c.** How many times before the six turned up? ☐

*Visual Text*

## Downtown Zoo

## Understanding

Shade the bubble that best answers each question.

**a.** How will you find the animals?
- ◯ go straight ahead
- ◯ follow the paths
- ◯ by going to the right
- ◯ by going to the left

**b.** When will you be able to see Koalas?
- ◯ in the morning
- ◯ before lunch
- ◯ in the afternoon
- ◯ at any time during the day

**c.** How many ducks will you see?
- ◯ one
- ◯ three
- ◯ five
- ◯ seven

**d.** What colour is the kangaroo?
- ◯ red
- ◯ grey
- ◯ white
- ◯ brown

**e.** Where are you likely to see the kangaroo?
- ◯ in a cage
- ◯ anywhere
- ◯ near the entrance
- ◯ nowhere

## Interpreting

Write an answer for each question.

**a.** How much will it cost for mum and you to enter the zoo? ______________________

**b.** Does the zoo welcome visitors? Circle Yes or No.

**c.** When would you see the reptiles? ______________________

**d.** Can you buy lunch at the zoo? ______________________

## Language: Common and Proper Nouns

***Common Nouns:*** name objects. ***Proper Nouns:*** Name people and places and use a capital letter.

**1.** Underline the proper noun in the following list.

**reptiles** **kangaroo** **Downtown Zoo** **diamond python**

**2.** Use the proper noun in this sentence.

**a.** The name of the zoo is ______________________.

**b.** Because it is a name it is a ______________________ noun.

## Spelling

Look, cover, write, check each word.

- enjoy ____________ ☐
- follow ____________ ☐
- seniors ____________ ☐
- animals ____________ ☐
- monkeys ____________ ☐
- reptiles ____________ ☐
- separate ____________ ☐
- entrance ____________ ☐
- renovate ____________ ☐
- kangaroo ____________ ☐

## Word Building

Words ending in '**y**' change to '**i**' when adding '**ness**'.

happy ____________ pretty ____________

funny ____________ silly ____________

naughty ____________

Words ending in '**y**' keep the '**y**' when adding '**ing**'.

cry ____________ try ____________

buy ____________ say ____________

enjoy ____________

## Sentences: Verbs must agree with their Subject.

Read each sentence, circle the correct verb in brackets and underline the word it is helping.

**helping verbs:** am, is, are, was, were

**a.** There (is / are) standing room only on the bus.
**b.** We (is / are) going to see the koala after lunch.
**c.** I (is / am) looking at the reptiles before lunch.
**d.** Children under 10 (was / were) getting free rides.
**e.** Everyone (was / were) having a great day out!

## Number Patterns

**1.** Write the missing number in each pattern.

**a.** 350, 400, 450, ____________ ,550

**b.** 1725, 1750, ____________ ,1800,1825

**2.** Write the number **before** and **after** each of these.

**a.** ____________ 8369 ____________

**b.** ____________ 7000 ____________

**2.** Order these numbers **smallest** to **largest**.

8316, 5628, 3915, 9742, 8314

____________________________________________

## Fractions

**1.** Colour in each shape the given fraction.

**a.**  $\frac{3}{4}$

**b.**  $\frac{1}{4}$

**2.** Colour the number of objects to match the fraction.

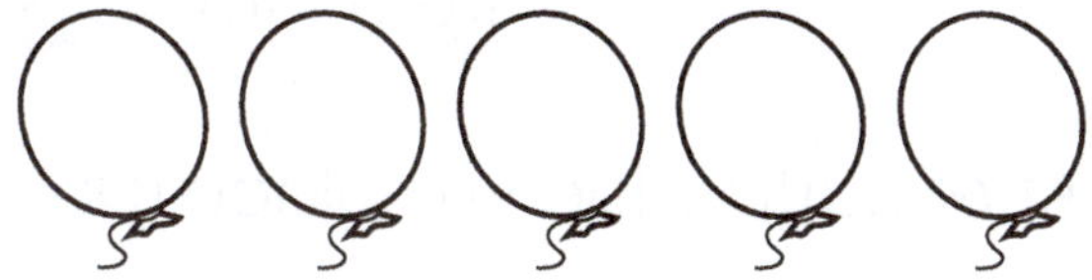 $\frac{4}{5}$

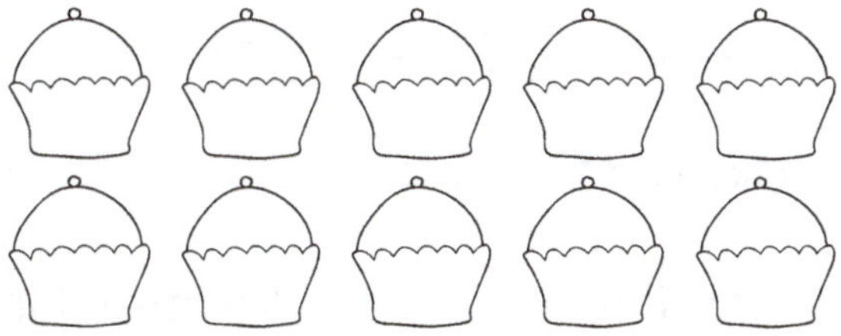 $\frac{3}{10}$

## Fresh Fruit Salad

What you will need:

1 only of the following fruits -
an orange, an apple, a pear & a banana
2 only Passionfruit
A Salad Bowl
Ice-cream, yoghurt or fresh cream
A knife to peel and cut the fruit

Instructions:

1. Peel the fruit and then cut each piece into small bites.
2. Place the fruit into the bowl and mix with the passionfruit.
3. Serve in small dishes with your choice of ice-cream, yoghurt or fresh cream.

## Understanding

Circle **Yes** or **No** to answer each question.

| | | |
|---|---|---|
| a. Would you be able to make this fruit salad? | Yes | No |
| b. Do you think the fruit salad would be a healthy choice? | Yes | No |
| c. Will you need to keep this salad in the 'fridge? | Yes | No |
| d. Would large bites make the salad more edible? | Yes | No |
| e. Could you make this for your dinner? | Yes | No |

## Interpreting

**a.** What does the word **edible** mean? Tick your choice.

◯ suitable ◯ fresh ◯ fit to eat ◯ ripe

**b.** Why is the word **'fridge'** written with an apostrophe?

◯ to shorten the word ◯ because it is cold
◯ for effect ◯ to show part of the word is missing

**c.** How much fruit would you use for this salad?

◯ three pieces ◯ four pieces ◯ five pieces ◯ six pieces

**d.** Give one word for **"What you will need"**

◯ ingredients ◯ directions ◯ orders ◯ require

## Language

Fill in the sentences using a suitable adjective from the list below.

fresh small salad each small

a. After cutting the fruit place it into a ________________ bowl.

b. ____________ piece needs to be cut into ______________ bites.

c. Make sure only ________________ cream is used.

d. When it is served it looks great in ____________ dishes.

## Spelling

Look, cover, write, check each word.

bowl ____________________ ☐

peel ____________________ ☐

orange ____________________ ☐

banana ____________________ ☐

fruit ____________________ ☐

serve ____________________ ☐

cream ____________________ ☐

yoghurt ____________________ ☐

passion ____________________ ☐

knife ____________________ ☐

## Word Building

**ou** and **ow** words – sounds like **our**
Complete each word -

c ________ h ________ n ________

pr ______d pl ______gh b ______gh

cr ______n dr______n h ______l

Here are some **ow** words with an **o** sound.

| | | |
|---|---|---|
| **bowl** | **grow** | **show** |
| **mow** | **flow** | **own** |

Write three different **ow** words.

__________ __________ __________

## Sentences: Independent Clauses and Main Ideas

Underline the main idea in each sentence.

**a.** We went to town to buy groceries.
**b.** Mum and I had lunch at the café.
**c.** When we were finished, we caught the bus home.
**d.** Do you know how to get to the football game?
**e.** There will be no rain if the weather stays like this.

## Capacity

Write the most appropriate unit - millilitre (**mL**) or litre (**L**).

**1.** 

250______

**2.** 

6______

**3.** 

60______

**4.** 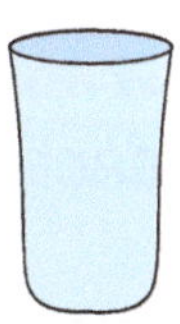

300______

**5.** 

5______

**6.** 

100______

## Symmetry

**1.** Draw the other half of each capital letter.

**a.** 

**b.** 

**c.** 

**2.** Draw the other half of this t-shirt then colour it red.

### Telephone Calls

To use the phone to call your friends
What you do is follow the trends.
This might be to push each number
Or just remember one single number.

For on your phone you can store
Any number you'll need for sure,
And there it will be for you to use,
Whenever there is important news.

To share with your friends and family,
And maybe also your grandma and me!
But don't be long because your calls for free
Will soon be gone and unhappy you'll be!

**Understanding** Use the poem to write an answer.

**a.** What is the main message in the first verse?

______________________________

**b.** Why does the poet say you will be unhappy?

______________________________

**c.** What can you share with your friends?

______________________________

**d.** Is there an easy way to remember phone numbers?

______________________________

**e.** Write the meaning of 'trends' in this poem?

______________________________

**Interpreting** Circle **Yes** or **No** to answer each question.

| | | |
|---|---|---|
| **a.** Would it be wise to stay on the phone for a long time? | Yes | No |
| **b.** Are telephone calls expensive? | Yes | No |
| **c.** Does it cost a lot to make a mobile phone call? | Yes | No |
| **d.** Should children your age have a mobile phone? | Yes | No |
| **e.** Do you have your own mobile phone? | Yes | No |

**Language** **1.** Write an **action** verb to complete each clause.

**a.** ____________the trends. **b.** ____________your friends.

**c.** ____________each number. **d.** ____________the phone.

**2.** Circle the **action** verbs in this story.

The car swung carelessly around the corner. It raced along the freeway. People ran from every direction. They called the police who arrived quickly.

## Spelling

Look, cover, write, check each word.

- friends ______ ☐
- follow ______ ☐
- might ______ ☐
- remember ______ ☐
- number ______ ☐
- whenever ______ ☐
- important ______ ☐
- family ______ ☐
- because ______ ☐
- member ______ ☐

## Word Building

**Synonyms** – Words that mean the same.
Write list words that mean the same as:

- pals ______
- an amount ______
- related ______
- maybe ______
- recall ______

Write the compound words in the poem as two words.

______

______

## Sentences: Conjunctions

Join the two clauses using "**and**" or "**but**" without repeating the pronoun.

**a.** My phone is blue. My phone is an iPhone.

______

**b.** I need more credit. I have to save some money first.

______

**c.** We were having a picnic. We left too late.

______

## Vertical Addition

**1.** Add the numbers vertically.

**a.**

| | H | T | O |
|---|---|---|---|
| | 7 | 2 | 3 |
| + | 1 | 4 | 6 |
| | | | |

**b.**

| | H | T | O |
|---|---|---|---|
| | 6 | 3 | 4 |
| + | 2 | 4 | 5 |
| | | | |

**c.**

| | TH | H | T | O |
|---|---|---|---|---|
| | 3 | 7 | 1 | 3 |
| + | 1 | 2 | 5 | 5 |
| | | | | |

**d.**

| | TH | H | T | O |
|---|---|---|---|---|
| | 4 | 5 | 2 | 3 |
| + | 1 | 3 | 5 | 3 |
| | | | | |

**2.** Samira had $235 and her sister had $243. How much did the girls have altogether?

| | H | T | O |
|---|---|---|---|
| | 2 | 3 | 5 |
| + | 2 | 4 | 3 |
| | | | |

They had $ ______ in total.

## Angles

**1.** Colour the **right angles**. Test the angles with the corner of a book. Tick the acute angles.

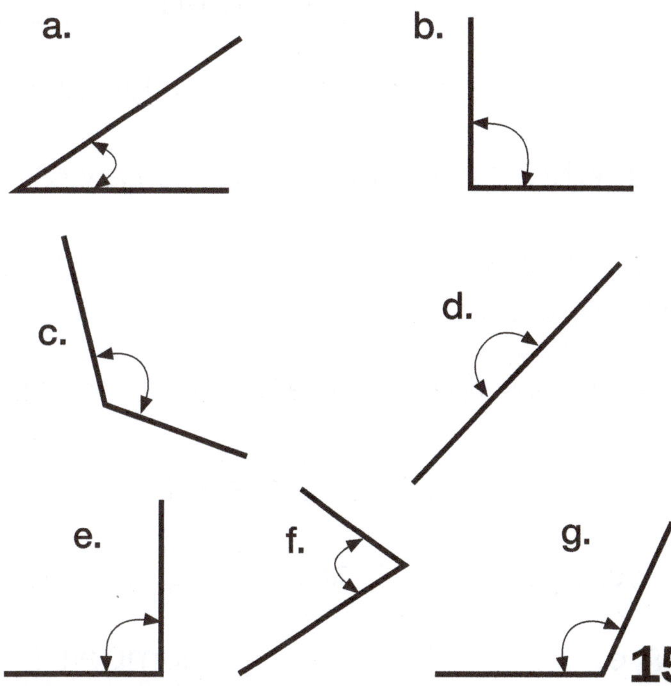

**The Local Grocery Shop**

This shop is located in the main street of Smithtown. It has very large windows with yellow and blue banners across the front of each window. Above the entrance door is a sign which reads:

Mr Bert New – Proprietor.

Above the sign, in big, bold numbers, is 2008. The name of the shop is Food 4 All and this is written in tall, black letters on each window. The shop front is inviting, clean and well lit. Mr New is a cheerful man, who often stands on the foot path to greet people.

## Understanding

Colour the picture below to show your understanding of this description.

## Interpreting

Write an answer to each question.

**a.** Who owns the shop? ____________________

**b.** Where is the shop located? ____________________

**c.** Name the type of shop in this description. ____________________

**d.** What might one expect to buy at the shop? ____________________

**e.** When was this shop built? ____________________

## Language

Use the descriptions above to find missing adjectives or nouns. Write (**A**) adjectives or (**N**) nouns.

**a.** ____________ street ( )

**b.** very large ____________ ( )

**c.** ________ and ________ banners ( )

**d.** ____________ door ( )

**e.** ________ ________ numbers ( )

**f.** ________ ________ letters ( )

## Spelling

Look, cover, write, check each word.

- grocer ____________ ☐
- locate ____________ ☐
- yellow ____________ ☐
- window ____________ ☐
- sign ____________ ☐
- narrow ____________ ☐
- written ____________ ☐
- maintain ____________ ☐
- cheerful ____________ ☐
- greeting ____________ ☐

## Word Building

**Antonyms:** Words that mean the opposite.
Write the opposite in meaning to:

- narrow ____________
- unhappy ____________
- summer ____________
- first ____________
- before ____________
- beginning ____________
- black ____________
- young ____________

## Sentences

Rewrite each sentence using the correct punctuation.

**a.** our shoes are red black blue and brown

____________________________________________

**b.** was there a bright yellow round ball on the field

____________________________________________

**c.** the colours of the rainbow are red orange yellow green blue indigo and violet

____________________________________________

## Vertical Subtraction

**1.** Subtract numbers to complete each algorithm.

**a.**

| | H | T | O |
|---|---|---|---|
| | 6 | 8 | 3 |
| - | 3 | 2 | 2 |
| | | | |

**b.**

| | H | T | O |
|---|---|---|---|
| | 4 | 9 | 5 |
| - | 1 | 7 | 1 |
| | | | |

**c.**

| | H | T | O |
|---|---|---|---|
| | 8 | 6 | 5 |
| - | 3 | 3 | 1 |
| | | | |

**d.**

| | H | T | O |
|---|---|---|---|
| | 6 | 9 | 2 |
| - | 3 | 3 | 0 |
| | | | |

**2.** Paris has 184 apps on her iPad. She deleted 122 of them. How many did she have left?

☐ – ☐ = ☐

## Location

Give the position of the groceries found on the supermarket shelf.

**1.** Name the grocery item to the **right** of the soft drink. ____________

**2.** What grocery item is directly **above** the coffee? ____________

## Should People Have Dogs?

I firmly believe that dogs are an important part of everybody's life. Without a dog, life would be empty for many people.

Take for instance the blind. Dogs are trained to be guides for people without sight. Therefore, they become just like another part of the blind person and are necessary for them in their daily lives. Without a guide dog many people cannot even cross the road safely or move about streets and shops. That is why, I believe, the dog is a wonderful companion and helper for these people.

Some dogs have been known to save their owner's life. A dog will fend off snakes, follow the scent of a lost child, stay with a lost child until help arrives and even keep the child warm overnight in cold weather.

Dogs are very clever and can find their way home after many months away. Army dogs are trained to sniff out dangerous weapons and save soldiers' lives. One brave army dog went missing for twelve months, because he was frightened by an explosion. Upon his return to base camp his handler was surprised! No doubt, by now, you will agree with me that people should have a dog at home or at work.

### Understanding

Underline the best answer to each question.

1. Which is the best reason for having a dog?
   ◯ it can be playful. ◯ A dog is clever. ◯ It gives joy to its owner. ◯ It is important
2. How do dogs help blind people?
   ◯ They keep them safe. ◯ Dogs help them do jobs.
   ◯ They play with them. ◯ Dogs bark a lot.

### Interpreting

1. Write two ways dogs can save lives.

   a. ______________________ b. ______________________
2. Write the meaning of "a wonderful companion"
   ______________________
3. Who would be the dog's 'handler'? ______________________
4. Where might the 'base camp' be? ______________________

### Language

***Singular Pronouns:*** I, me, you, he, she ***Plural Pronouns:*** we, us, you, them, they

Re-write the sentence in bold, using a personal pronoun to avoid repeating the noun.

a. Hal was sick today. **Hal stayed in bed.**
______________________

b. Sue went to the show. **Sue bought a show bag.**
______________________

c. Ali and Sam are in the park. **Ali and Sam are on the swings.**
______________________

## Spelling

Look, cover, write, check each word.

firmly ____________ ☐

important ____________ ☐

empty ____________ ☐

guide ____________ ☐

instance ____________ ☐

therefore ____________ ☐

necessary ____________ ☐

companion ____________ ☐

weather ____________ ☐

dangerous ____________ ☐

## Word Building

Form plural of nouns ending in '**f**' by changing '**f**' to '**v**' and add '**es**' eg. loaf, loaves. Change these to plurals.

calf ____________ wolf ____________

shelf ____________ leaf ____________

thief ____________ loaf ____________

Circle the incorrect words.

**a.** Teh tres leves are green.

**b.** Hour caves are one our old.

**c.** Dog are gud kumpanny.

## Sentences

Complete the sentences with an appropriate persuasive device.

I firmly believe | could | I think | because | if | you will agree | should

**a.** Training is tonight ____________ we must be ready for Saturday's game.

**b.** We ____________ win this game ____________ we train hard all week.

**c.** That is what ____________ and I hope ____________ .

**d.** What ____________ you ____________ do is try your best to win.

## Tables

| | | | |
|---|---|---|---|
| 2x0=0 | 3x0=0 | 5x0=0 | 10x0=0 |
| 2x1=2 | 3x1=3 | 5x1=5 | 10x1=10 |
| 2x2=4 | 3x2=6 | 5x2=10 | 10x2=20 |
| 2x3=6 | 3x3=9 | 5x3=15 | 10x3=30 |
| 2x4=8 | 3x4=12 | 5x4=20 | 10x4=40 |
| 2x5=10 | 3x5=15 | 5x5=25 | 10x5=50 |
| 2x6=12 | 3x6=18 | 5x6=30 | 10x6=60 |
| 2x7=14 | 3x7=21 | 5x7=35 | 10x7=70 |
| 2x8=16 | 3x8=24 | 5x8=40 | 10x8=80 |
| 2x9=18 | 3x9=27 | 5x9=45 | 10x9=90 |
| 2x10=20 | 3x10=30 | 5x10=50 | 10x10=100 |

**1.** Fill in the missing numbers.

**a.** ☐ × 5 = 45 **b.** ☐ × 3 = 27

**c.** ☐ × 5 = 35 **d.** ☐ × 10 = 70

## Multiplication

**1.** Write the number sentence for each number line.

**a.**

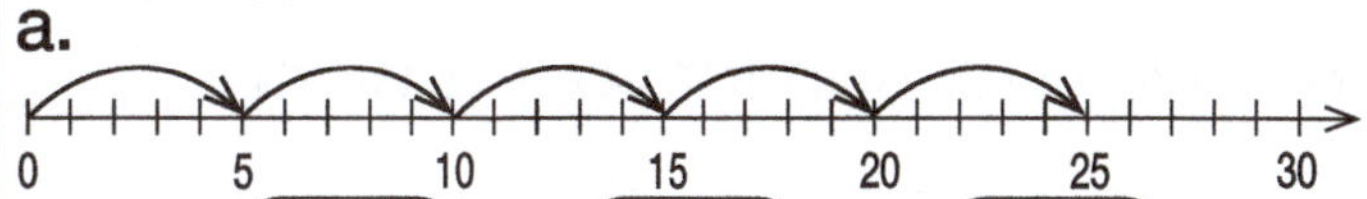


☐ x ☐ = ☐

**b.**

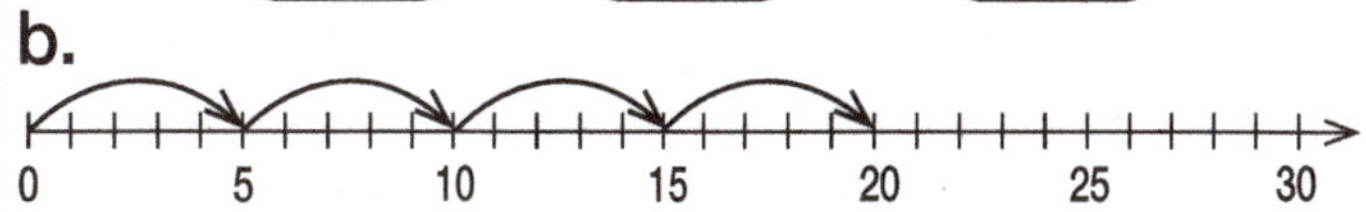


☐ x ☐ = ☐

**2.** Write the product of each set of factors.

**a.** 2 × 5 = ☐ **b.** 5 × 9 = ☐

**c.** 3 × 5 = ☐ **d.** 3 × 10 = ☐

**Tim's Roadhouse Café**

| | |
|---|---|
| Sandwiches | |
| Ham, Cheese and Tomato | 5.50 |
| Chicken, Avocado and Lettuce | 6.00 |
| Egg and Lettuce | 3.50 |
| Cheese, Vegemite and Lettuce | 3.00 |
| Extras: Tomato, Cucumber, Onion, Relish, Sauces | 0.50 each |
| Hot Food | |
| Bacon and Eggs (fried, scrambled or poached) | 10.00 |
| Fish and Chips | 9.00 |
| Hamburgers - Plain | 7.00 |
| - The Works (Bacon, Egg, Tomato...) | 10.50 |
| Cold Drinks - as marked | |
| Hot Drinks - available on request. (Tea, Coffee) from | 4.00 |
| In either a cup or mug | |

## Understanding

Underline, or write, the best answer to each question.

**1.** Which would be cheaper to buy?

**a.** An Egg Sandwich; **b.** A Plain Hamburger **c.** Fish and Chips **d.** Bacon and Eggs

**2.** Which item of food is the dearest to buy? ____________________

**3.** Which items on the menu cost the same? ____________________

**4.** How much would a plain hamburger with tea cost? ____________________

## Interpreting

Write your answer to each question.

**a.** Where might you find this roadhouse? ____________________

**b.** Give a reason for your answer. ____________________

**c.** What is meant by drink price 'as marked'? ____________________

**d.** Why do you think there is not a big selection of food on the menu?

____________________

## Language

Choose a noun or noun group from the menu to complete each sentence.

**a.** We bought ____________ and ____________ for nine ____________ .

**b.** For three dollars, I had a ________, ________ and ____________ sandwich.

**c.** Dad enjoyed a ____________ ____________ for $10.50.

**d.** Mum wanted a ________ of ____________ and paid the four ____________ .

**e.** I asked for scrambled ____________ and a cold ____________ .

## Spelling

Look, cover, write, check each word.

sandwich ____________ ☐
cheese ____________ ☐
tomato ____________ ☐
avocado ____________ ☐
lettuce ____________ ☐
vegemite ____________ ☐
onion ____________ ☐
bacon ____________ ☐
available ____________ ☐
poached ____________ ☐

## Word Building

### Compound Words

| Add **under** | Add **day** |
|---|---|
| ________ neath | birth ________ |
| ________ ground | Sun ________ |
| ________ line | week ________ |
| ________ stood | every ________ |

Rule: Add **es** to words ending in **o** for plural.

tomato ____________

dingo ____________

potato ____________

## Sentences

Add inverted commas to each sentence to show what has been said.

**a.** Bring me back an egg and lettuce sandwich please.

____________________________________________

**b.** These fish and chips are hot cried Josie.

____________________________________________

**c.** I just love these bacon and eggs said dad.

____________________________________________

## Division

**1.** How many equal groups of 3 can be made from this array?

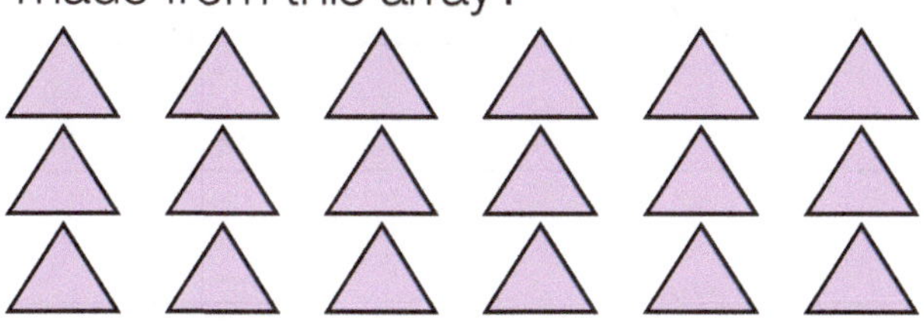

☐ ÷ ☐ = ☐

**2.** How many groups of two in 20? ☐

**3.** How many groups of three in 24? ☐

**4.** How many groups of five in 45? ☐

## Division

**5.** Share 30 blue counters equally into five groups.

☐ ☐ ☐ ☐ ☐

**6. PROBLEM:**
There was $24 to be equally shared between three children. How much did each one receive?

☐ ÷ ☐ = ☐

## My Day at the Zoo

Yesterday I went to the new zoo near my place. It only opened two weeks ago.

While I was there I saw the red pandas being fed. They didn't want to move out of their tree for the keeper, because it was too hot. So, the lady who was feeding them, went to them and gave them fruit and vegetables on a stick. It is important for them to eat twice a day to keep healthy.

Then I went and saw the snow leopards. These are beautiful creatures but they weren't as white as I thought they would be. I guess that's because they were not in the snow! However, they can live in temperatures ranging from - 40 to + 40 degrees.

After that I walked around and saw a lot of Australian animals. There was the Eastern Grey Kangaroo and a lot of Wallaroos having a rest. The Emu was walking back and forth and the water ducks were weaving in and out of its way.

The endangered black-handed spider monkey was busy swinging from rope to rope. It came right over close to me and looked me right in the eye. I thought it was a sticky-beak!

Last of all I visited the koala sanctuary. There were many koalas in the zoo but they were asleep in special types of eucalypt trees and only came down for a feed. I patted one before I left.

### Understanding

Find answers to the following

**a.** What was walking back and forth? ____________________

**b.** How did the monkeys move? ____________________

**c.** Why are the monkeys called 'sticky-beaks'? ____________________

**d.** Which animal was not keen to eat? Why? ____________________

**e.** How long has anyone been able to visit this zoo? ____________________

### Interpreting

Find the meaning of the following words. You might need to use a dictionary.

**a.** sanctuary ____________________ **b.** endangered ____________________

**c.** Where do snow leopards mostly live? ____________________

**d.** Where do eucalypt trees grow? ____________________

**e.** How long each day does the koala sleep? ____________________

### Language

Select a word from the word bank that best describes each given noun.

snow    eucalypt    red    eastern grey    black-handed spider

**a.** ____________ trees **b.** ____________ pandas **c.** ____________ leopard

**d.** ____________ kangaroo **e.** ____________ monkeys

## Spelling

Look, cover, write, check each word.

- yesterday ____________________ ☐
- vegetables ____________________ ☐
- healthy ____________________ ☐
- leopard ____________________ ☐
- beautiful ____________________ ☐
- creature ____________________ ☐
- guess ____________________ ☐
- endanger ____________________ ☐
- eucalypt ____________________ ☐
- important ____________________ ☐

## Word Building

Add '**ly**' to form adverbs. Rewrite:

- quick ____________________
- slow ____________________
- soft ____________________
- near ____________________
- quiet ____________________
- real ____________________
- beautiful ____________________
- important ____________________
- final ____________________

## Sentences: Adverbs - Tell how, when, where, why

Underline the adverbs in each sentence.

**a.** We arrived yesterday, but it was too wet to go out.
**b.** The flowers were beautifully arranged, on the table.
**c.** We ran above the river, but beneath the bridge.
**d.** After Friday, we are going away, because it's holiday time.
**e.** Before very long, the snow leopards came into sight.

## Data

This graph shows how children travel to school. Use the graph to answer the questions.

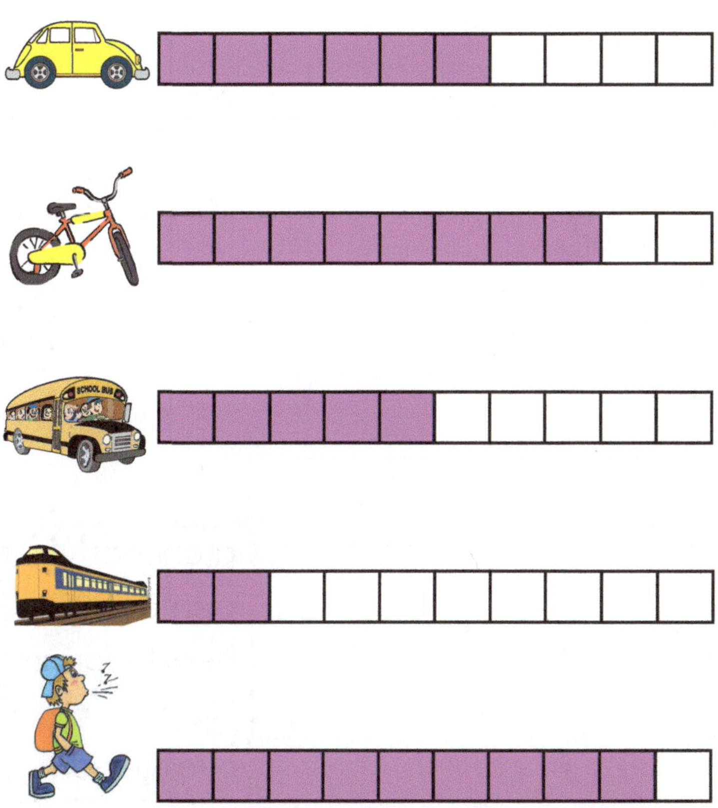

## Data

1. How many children walk to school? ☐
2. How many ride their bikes to school? ☐
3. What is the **least** popular form of travel to school? ____________
4. How many more children come to school by bike than by bus? ☐
5. How many children arrive at school by car? ☐
6. How many more children walk than come by car? ☐
7. How many children are represented on the graph? ☐

## The Pentagon

This is the most famous, five-sided shaped building in the World. It is in Arlington, Virginia and sits across the Potomac (Po-toe-mac) River from Washington, DC, the capital of the USA. Because of its size, it's almost a city in itself.

George Bergstrom was the architect who designed the Pentagon, which was built during the Second World War, from 1941 to 1943. The headquarters of the American Department of Defense is located there and all military records are kept there.

The building has reinforced concrete outer walls, to make it hard to destroy by fire. Because of its design, when one of the four aeroplanes, hijacked in the terrorist attack on America in 2001, flew into the Pentagon only that one part of the building was destroyed. That section has since been re-built.

The Pentagon is said to hold the biggest library of war history in the World. Intelligence and information about foreign countries can be sourced there too.

### Understanding

Write the best answer to each question.

**a.** Why is the word Potomac written in brackets? ____________________

**b.** How long did it take to build the Pentagon? ____________________

**c.** What is the capital of the USA? ____________________

**d.** When was the terrorist attack on America? ____________________

**e.** How many aeroplanes flew into the Pentagon? ____________________

### Interpreting

Write a response to each question.

**a.** What prevented more parts of the building from being destroyed?

____________________

**b.** What is the meaning of the words 'sourced there'?

____________________

**c.** Why was the Pentagon built?

____________________

**d.** Write another meaning for 'sits across the ... river'.

____________________

### Language

Match the technical word from the word bank to its meaning.

**a.** Gathering secret information ____________________

**b.** Centre of operations ____________________

**c.** To take by threat or force ____________________

**d.** Designer of buildings ____________________

**e.** Five-sided building ____________________

| Word bank |
| --- |
| architect |
| pentagon |
| headquarters |
| hijack |
| intelligence |

## Spelling

## Unit 11

Look, cover, write, check each word.

famous ____________________ ☐

because ____________________ ☐

size ____________________ ☐

built ____________________ ☐

defend ____________________ ☐

defensive ____________________ ☐

record ____________________ ☐

concrete ____________________ ☐

section ____________________ ☐

history ____________________ ☐

## Word Building

When 'full' is used as a suffix one 'l' is dropped. Eg. hope + full = hopeful

Write each word adding 'full'.

hand+full ____________________

use+full ____________________

mind+full ____________________

care+full ____________________

hope+full ____________________

truth+full ____________________

shame+full ____________________

## Sentences: Capital Letters for Titles and Forms of Address

Rewrite the following sentences using capital letters and full stops where needed.

**a.** mr spring and mrs summer were going on holidays

____________________________________________

**b.** the department of defense is in america note how america spells defense

____________________________________________

**c.** in australia we have a governor general who represents queen elizabeth

____________________________________________

## Money and Change

Write the value for each group of coins.

**a.**

☐

**b.**

☐

**c.** Write this sum of money in words.

$2.75 ____________________

____________________

## Division and Multiplication

**1.** Complete each number sentence.

**a.** $20 \div 5 =$ ☐ **b.** $24 \div 3 =$ ☐

**c.** $40 \div 5 =$ ☐ **d.** $14 \div 2 =$ ☐

**e.** $18 \div 2 =$ ☐ **f.** $18 \div 3 =$ ☐

**2.** Complete each multiplication sentence.

**a.** $3 \times 7 =$ ☐ **b.** $2 \times 8 =$ ☐

**c.** $5 \times 6 =$ ☐ **d.** $5 \times 9 =$ ☐

**e.** $2 \times 30 =$ ☐ **f.** $3 \times 11 =$ ☐

## Should iPads be used in Schools?

First of all, I believe that there is a place for the iPad in school, because information can be found using them and this, in turn, can be used to make learning easier.

Then as you know, a student might not be able to find what is needed in a book and it certainly won't be as interesting.
Also, information changes too and up-to-date information may not always be in a book but it can be very current from the iPad.

However, on the other hand, not all students might have access to an iPad and that means they won't be able to find out as much as some others can.
In which case, an iPad will be of no advantage to students and they will need to rely on some other way to learn.

What I believe would be the best for all students, is for schools to provide an iPad for everyone to use. Then there will be an equal opportunity for everyone to experience learning using this new technology.

### Understanding

Write **1-5** to order these arguments from the text.

**a.** Everyone will have the same opportunity to learn. ________

**b.** You might not find information in a book. ________

**c.** Some students might not be able to buy an iPad. ________

**d.** The school should provide each student with an iPad. ________

**e.** It will be easier to find up-to-date information using an iPad. ________

### Interpreting

Write the meaning of these words as used in the text.

**a.** advantage ________ **b.** equal opportunity ________

**c.** provide ________ **d.** current ________

**e.** access ________ **f.** rely ________

**g.** certainly ________ **h.** technology ________

### Language

**1.** Underline the persuasive language in the following text.

From the beginning I believed it was important for everyone to have an iPad. Why should only a few students have them? If it is too expensive for some students to buy their own then the school can and should, raise the money to buy one for everyone. Don't you agree?

**2.** Write your response in favour of this argument here:

________

________

# Unit 12

## Spelling

Look, cover, write, check each word.

- believe ______ ☐
- certain ______ ☐
- change ______ ☐
- access ______ ☐
- advantage ______ ☐
- rely ______ ☐
- experience ______ ☐
- everyone ______ ☐
- should ______ ☐
- information ______ ☐

## Word Building

Words ending in **ay, ey, oy,** just add '**s**' to make them plural. Eg. day, days.

Follow the rule to write the plural of:

- play ______
- key ______
- toy ______
- relay ______
- valley ______
- convoy ______
- monkey ______

## Sentences: Prepositions to begin Adverbial Phrases

Underline the adverbial phrase or phrases in each sentence and then write it on the line.

**a.** Mum went shopping on Tuesday. ______

**b.** We were home before dark. ______

**c.** After lunch there was time to play. ______

**d.** Every day in summer the team trained hard. ______

**e.** Through the bush ran the kangaroos. ______

## Angles

**1.** Label each angle as acute, obtuse, reflex, or right angle.

**a.** 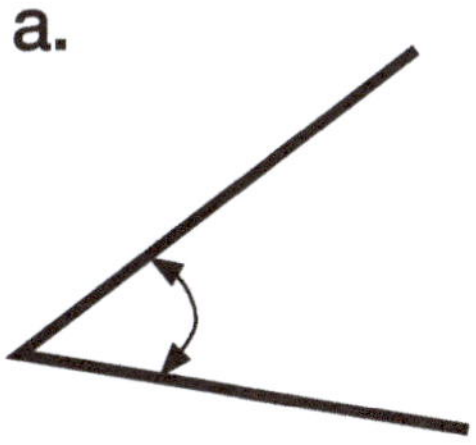 ______

**b.** 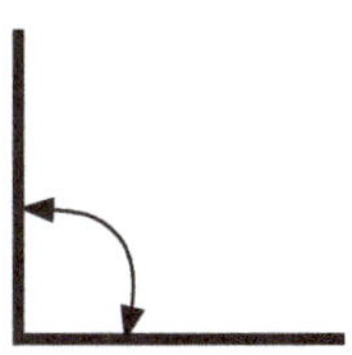 ______

**c.** 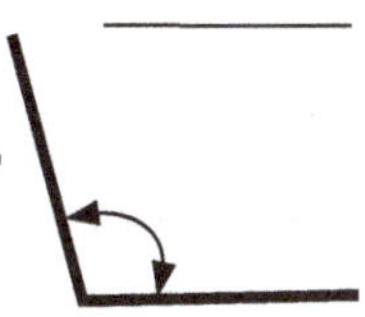 ______

**d.** 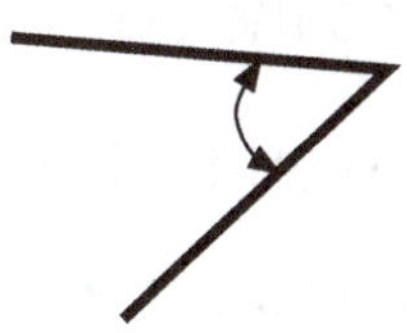 ______

**e.** 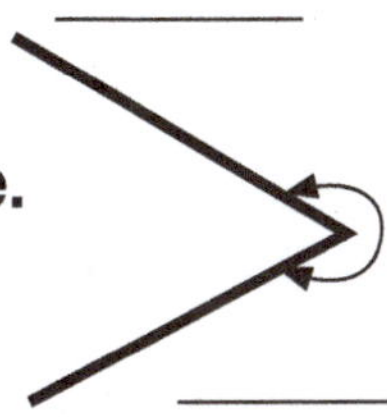 ______

**f.** 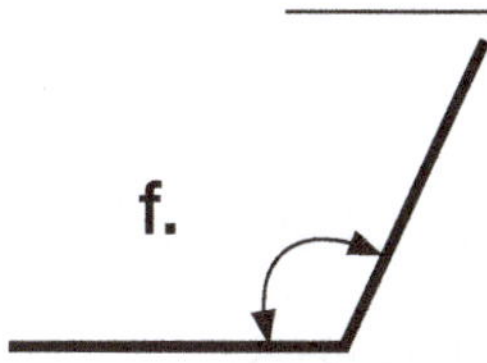 ______

## Time to the Minute

**1.** Write the times shown on the clock.

**a.** 

**b.** 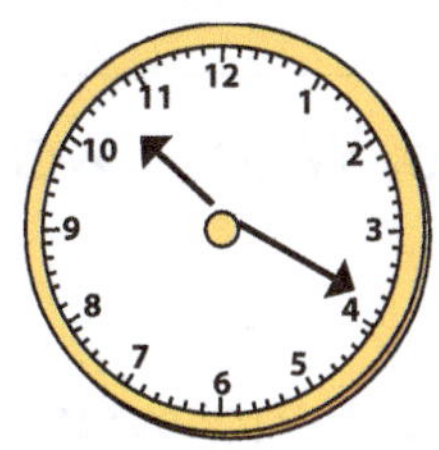


**2.** Match the digital times to written time.

**a.** 

**b.** 

**c.** 

**d.** Twenty five to seven

**e.** Quarter to ten

**f.** Quarter past three

## Reading

Match the historical event to its date and then order each event on the timeline.

| Historical Event | Date |
|---|---|
| **1.** The Arrival of the First Fleet | 1901 |
| **2.** Beginning of World War I | 1851 |
| **3.** Captain Cook and the Endeavour | 1788 |
| **4.** Gold was discovered in Australia | 1945 |
| **5.** Federation of Australia | 1770 |
| **6.** End of World War II | 1914 |

| | | | | | | |
|---|---|---|---|---|---|---|
| Number: | | | | | | |
| Date: | | | | | | |

## Understanding

Circle **Yes** or **No** to answer each question.

| | | |
|---|---|---|
| **a.** Do all of the events relate to happenings in Australia? | Yes | No |
| **b.** Captain Cook was in charge of the First Fleet. | Yes | No |
| **c.** World War I began in Europe. | Yes | No |
| **d.** All the States and Territories form the Federation of Australia. | Yes | No |
| **e.** Captain Arthur Phillip was in charge of the First Fleet. | Yes | No |

## Interpreting

Write a sentence to answer each question.

**a.** What was the Endeavour?

______________________________

**b.** What is meant by "the First Fleet"?

______________________________

**c.** Where was gold first discovered in Australia?

______________________________

**d.** Who was Captain Cook?

______________________________

## Language

Circle the preposition and underline the adverb in each sentence.

**Remember:** Prepositions come before a noun and adverbs come after a noun.

**a.** In town, we saw a band happily playing Jazz.

**b.** Towards me came the group slowly.

**c.** For fun, they all joined John with great excitement.

**d.** At dawn, the boats were sinking inside the reef.

## Spelling

Look, cover, write, check each word.

- history ____________ ☐
- historical ____________ ☐
- event ____________ ☐
- discover ____________ ☐
- discovered ____________ ☐
- federal ____________ ☐
- federation ____________ ☐
- arrive ____________ ☐
- arrival ____________ ☐
- Australia ____________ ☐

## Word Building

Nouns ending in **s,x,z,sh** and **ch** add '**es**' to make them plural. Eg. fox, foxes.

| | | | |
|---|---|---|---|
| kiss | ________ | cross | ________ |
| box | ________ | bus | ________ |
| buzz | ________ | pitch | ________ |
| bush | ________ | wish | ________ |
| beach | ________ | wax | ________ |
| grass | ________ | hatch | ________ |
| glass | ________ | fax | ________ |
| match | ________ | dux | ________ |

## Sentences

Join the following sentences using the correct conjunction from the list.

so that, so, because, since

**a.** Mary went to school. It was her birthday.

________________________________________

**b.** It was too wet to play sport. We stayed inside and read.

________________________________________

**c.** Dad has been riding a horse. He was eight years old.

________________________________________

**d.** We will buy the tickets. All of us will be together.

________________________________________

## Vertical Subtraction

**1.** Write the vertical subtraction for each set of blocks.

**a.**

| H | T | O |
|---|---|---|
| | | |
| - | | |
| | | |

**b.**

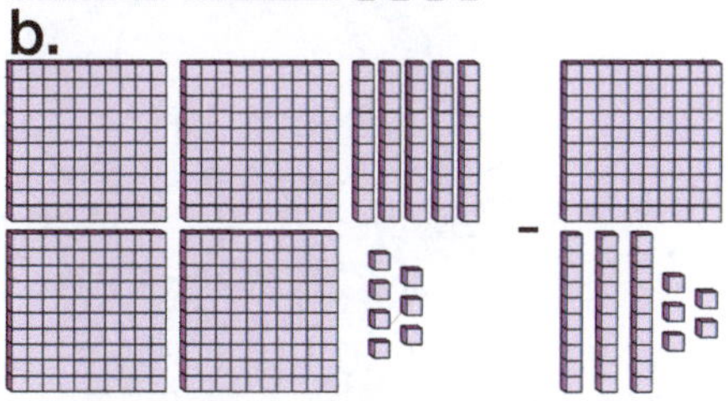

| H | T | O |
|---|---|---|
| | | |
| - | | |
| | | |

**2.** Write the algorithm for this subtraction sentence.

865 - 223 = ________

| H | T | O |
|---|---|---|
| | | |
| - | | |
| | | |

## Chance

Here are three bags of 3D objects.

If you take one object from each bag, colour the combination you are most likely to get.

**a.**

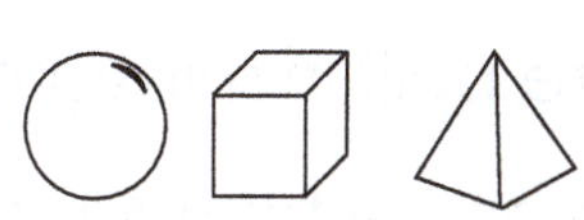

**b.**

**c.**

## Why Does a Ship Float?

A ship is a large object made of very heavy metal.
Why then does it float in the water and not sink to the bottom?

A ship is hollow so it pushes the water out of the way and it sits on top. The weight of the ship pushes the water and the water pushes back, with equal force, keeping the ship afloat. What it does is, it *displaces* the water.

This very old principle of water *displacement* was discovered by Archimedes, an ancient Greek.

## Understanding: True or False

After each of the following statements, write whether it is true or false.

a. Ships are made of steel. ____________________

b. Water swallows ships and they sink. ____________________

c. The force of the water keeps the ship afloat. ____________________

d. The weight of the water pushes the ship. ____________________

e. Water displacement was discovered a long time ago. ____________________

## Interpreting

Write another word for each one below.

a. metal ____________________ b. float ____________________

c. hollow ____________________ d. displace ____________________

e. weight ____________________ f. ancient ____________________

## Language

Circle the nouns and underline the noun groups in the following sentences.

a. The force of the water keeps the ship afloat.

b. The weight of the ship pushes the water.

c. Ships are built in shipyards around the World.

d. Sailors can be found in every Australian port.

e. I have sat for hours and watched the big ships glide into port.

f. Archimedes was an ancient Greek who discovered the principle of water displacement.

## Spelling

Look, cover, write, check each word.

metal ______________________ ☐

float ______________________ ☐

hollow ______________________ ☐

weight ______________________ ☐

equal ______________________ ☐

displace ______________________ ☐

displacement ______________________ ☐

principle ______________________ ☐

principal ______________________ ☐

ancient ______________________ ☐

## Word Building

**Homophones** - Words that sound alike but have different spelling. Eg. saw/sore.

Find the meaning of each word in your dictionary.

principle ______________________

principal ______________________

wait ______________________

weight ______________________

metal ______________________

mettle ______________________

## Sentences

Number each sentence to show the order in which the events happen.

**a.** Now it is raining and too late to go. ________

**b.** Yesterday we were going away. ________

**c.** By the afternoon it had begun to cloud over. ________

**d.** Dad bought new camping gear on Monday. ________

**e.** Everyone was ready to leave in the morning. ________

## Numbers to 10 000

**1.** Circle the **largest** number in each row.

**a.** 4638, 4863, 4386, 4368, 4836

**b.** 8756, 8657, 8567, 8765, 8675

**c.** 4982, 4829, 4928, 4892, 4298

**d.** 5463, 5364, 5436, 5634, 5346

**2.** Write each number as a numeral.

**a.** Four thousand, six hundred and seventy-five ________

**b.** Six thousand, two hundred and sixty-eight ________

**c.** Eight thousand, nine hundred and ninety-nine ________

## The Kilogram

Write the appropriate unit of mass for each object - gram (**g**) or kilogram (**kg**).

**a.** 

70 ________

**b.** 

6 ________

**c.** 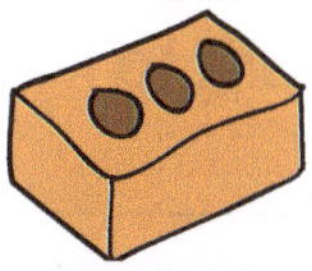

3 ________

**d.** 

700 ________

**e.** 

850 ________

**f.** 

3 ________

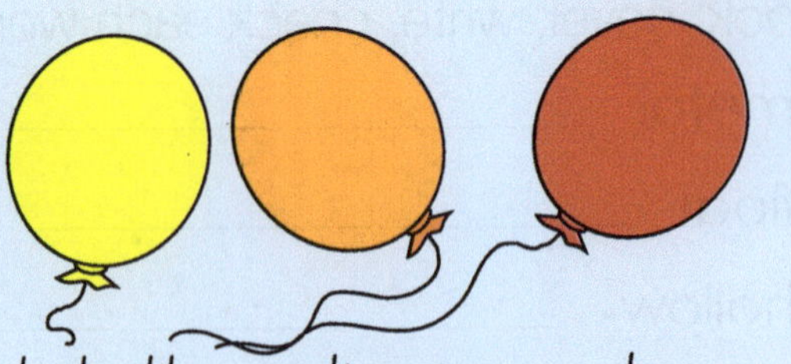

14 Rose Street,
Smithtown.
10 January 2015

Dear Sam

Thank you for the book you sent me for my birthday. I do like reading, as you know, and I particularly like Science books.
I have already tried a few of the experiments in the book and they have been fun. I particularly liked the one with the egg and the bottle. It is very easy to do and maybe our teacher will do it with the whole class soon. I shall ask her.
Let me know what you would like for your birthday. Send me an Email to let me know and I will get it next time mum takes me shopping.
Will you be having a birthday party this year? I didn't have one because it was too soon after Christmas and everyone I know was away on holidays. I will have one when I turn 10. The big '0'! That's what I heard mum say her next birthday will be. Gee! Don't forget to write soon so I will have time to get your present.

Cheers for now,
Patrick

## Understanding

Tick the bubble if you can find the information in the letter.

a. ◯ Sam received a birthday present.
b. ◯ The present was a book.
c. ◯ Patrick has written the letter.
d. ◯ Sam likes science experiments.
e. ◯ Sam's teacher will do experiments.
f. ◯ Sam's birthday is in December
g. ◯ Patrick didn't have a birthday party.
h. ◯ Patrick will be 10 on his birthday.
i. ◯ Patrick did some experiments.
j. ◯ Mum will have a 'big 0' birthday.

## Interpreting

Write a sentence to answer each question.

a. Why did Patrick write this letter?

______________________________

b. Write three important inclusions Patrick has in his letter.

______________________________

c. How does Patrick want Sam to let him know what he wants for his birthday?

______________________________

## Language

Circle the possessive pronoun in each sentence and then write it on the line.

a. That book is mine. ____________
b. I thought it was hers. ____________
c. This iPad is yours. ____________
d. Keep his score low. ____________
e. Those seats are theirs. ____________
f. The house is ours. ____________

## Spelling

Look, cover, write, check each word.

birthday ______________ ☐
already ______________ ☐
experiment ______________ ☐
whole ______________ ☐
hole ______________ ☐
holiday ______________ ☐
present ______________ ☐
after ______________ ☐
would ______________ ☐
wood ______________ ☐

## Word Building

Some words are always plural. Eg. scissors.
Match each word to its meaning.

trousers, pliers, glasses, slacks, scissors

cuts material ______________

bends wire ______________

worn by men ______________

used for seeing ______________

ladies pants ______________

Write two homophones in the list.

______________ ______________

## Sentences

Underline and then write the '**saying verbs**' in each sentence, on the line.

**a.** Paul whispered instructions to his classmates. ______________

**b.** "When will it be ready to eat?" Sam asked his mother. ______________

**c.** Everyone on the bus called out for the driver to stop! ______________

**d.** Can you tell me what happened in the playground? ______________

**e.** No one answered my call for help when I was hurt. ______________

## Length

**1.** Write metres (**m**) or centimetres (**cm**) for each object.

a. 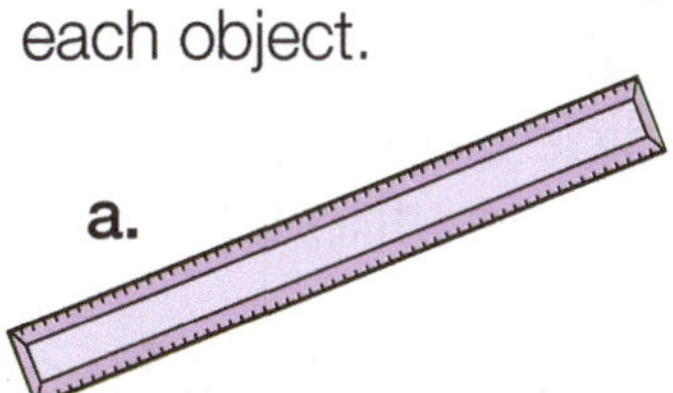

30 ______

b. 

4 ______

c. 

2 ______

d. 

21 ______

**2.** Draw a line across the page for the given length.

6cm

## Fractions

**1.** Colour the fractional part of each group.

a. $\frac{1}{3}$ 

b. $\frac{1}{2}$ 

**2.** Write what fraction is shaded in each shape.

a. 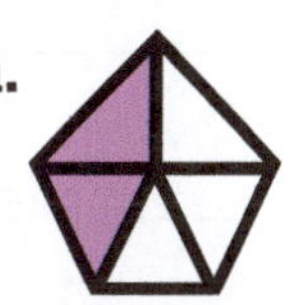 ___

b.  ___

c.  ___

d.  ___

*Disaster Awaits* was written by Kate Smart. It is the story of a young boy, Michael, and his family's ordeal to get him medical care while living in a remote country town north of Adelaide.

Michael needed regular trips to Adelaide for specialist treatment. Because it was too expensive to fly, the decision was made to drive there when necessary.

By car, the trip took 8 hours, one way. Starting before dawn, when it was cooler, Michael and his family would arrive in Adelaide by lunch time. It was during one of these trips south that everything that could go wrong did just that!

What happened and how the family survived their biggest challenge is at the centre of this story. Read the book to find out how the brave, young family overcame their biggest disaster.

## Understanding

Write a sentence to answer each question.

**a.** Why is the book titled *Disaster Awaits*?

______________________________

**b.** In which direction was Adelaide from the family home?

______________________________

**c.** Why did the family always drive to Adelaide?

______________________________

**d.** Who would be most likely to read this book? Why?

______________________________

## Interpreting

Shade the correct bubble to answer the question.

**a.** Why was the family going to Adelaide?

- ◯ to go shopping
- ◯ to visit grandparents
- ◯ to visit the doctor
- ◯ to go to the airport

**b.** Why did the family leave early each time?

- ◯ to drive the car
- ◯ to beat the heat
- ◯ to get to Adelaide on time
- ◯ to have time to enjoy the trip

**c.** At what time did the family leave home?

◯ 4 am ◯ 5 am ◯ 6 am

**d.** Which word is closest in meaning to 'ordeal'?

◯ pleasure ◯ delight ◯ difficulty ◯ happy

## Language

Complete these sentences using the correct article in the space.

**a.** When he ran towards __________ dam I saw ________ snake on the edge.

**b.** Everyone enjoys________ apple or________ egg but most of all I like______ peach.

**c.** After lunch we all had______ rest before having______ drink we brought with us.

## Spelling

Look, cover, write, check each word.

disaster ____________ ☐

ordeal ____________ ☐

medical ____________ ☐

regular ____________ ☐

expensive ____________ ☐

decision ____________ ☐

arrive ____________ ☐

happen ____________ ☐

survive ____________ ☐

wrong ____________ ☐

## Word Building

Most nouns ending in '**o**' add '**es**' in the plural.
Write the plural of each word.

tomato ____________

potato ____________

echo ____________

dingo ____________

hero ____________

volcano ____________

**But** for avocado just add '**s**'

avocado ____________

## Sentences: Complex Sentences

An independent (main) and a dependent clause form a complex sentence.
Underline the main clause and write the dependent clause from each sentence on the line.

**a.** Run fast, because it is raining. ____________

**b.** Before you wash, go to the letterbox. ____________

**c.** Undo the lock and then walk inside ____________

**d.** Repair your shoes while you can. ____________

**e.** Knowing how you can do it easily. ____________

## Subtraction

**1.** Subtract these numbers. Regroup the ones and tens column.

**a.**

| | T | O |
|---|---|---|
| | | |
| - | 8 | 2 |
| | 2 | 6 |
| | | |

**b.**

| | T | O |
|---|---|---|
| | | |
| - | 5 | 3 |
| | 1 | 5 |
| | | |

**c.**

| | T | O |
|---|---|---|
| | | |
| - | 9 | 4 |
| | 6 | 7 |
| | | |

**2.** Take the numbers around the wheel from the centre number.

## Width

**1.** Measure the length and height a $10 note.

☐ cm length ☐ cm height

**2.** Measure the length and height of each shape.

length ☐ cm

height ☐ cm

**3.** Find the perimeter of this shape. (Perimeter is the total measurement of all sides.)

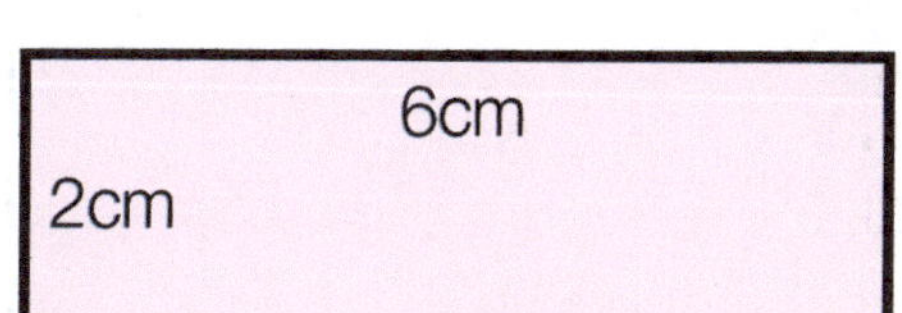


Perimeter = ☐ cm

**Index**

**Dewey Classification**

000 General
010 Philosophy & Psychology
200 Religions
220 Bible
300 Social Sciences
340 Law
370 Education
400 Languages
420 English & Old English
450 Italian language
500 Natural Sciences & Maths
550 Earth sciences
570 Life sciences
600 Technology
670 Manufacturing
690 Buildings
700 The Arts
720 Architecture
780 Music
800 Literature
810 American literature
890 Literature of other languages
900 Geography & History
910 Geography & travel
950 History of Asia, Far East
990 General history of other areas

## Organising a Library

*The Dewey Decimal Classification System* is used to decide where all non-fiction books are kept in a library. This system makes it easy to find any book, in any library. Even on the Internet.

All non-fiction books can be given a *Dewey* number and then a librarian will use the *Dewey Index* to be more specific about where it will fit under that number.

For example, a book about **motor cars** will be found on the 300s shelf, but to be more specific and to save time, it will be marked 388.3. That is how the Dewey System expands out amongst different categories.

## Understanding

Write an answer to each question.

**a.** Why do you think it is called the ***Dewey Decimal Classification System***?

______________________________

**b.** Who allocates books to a shelf in a library?

______________________________

**c.** What is used to be more specific about where a book goes on the shelf?

______________________________

**d.** Where will you find a book about **motor cars**?

______________________________

## Interpreting

Give each topic a Dewey Classification number.

**a.** Public Buildings ____________ **b.** The Beatles ____________

**c.** Arabic Languages ____________ **d.** Church History ____________

**e.** Education ____________ **f.** Tsunamis ____________

## Language

The reading has a number of technical words. Match each word to its meaning.

| Technical Word | Meaning |
|---|---|
| **a.** classification | **f.** one responsible for books in a library |
| **b.** non-fiction | **g.** putting like things together |
| **c.** librarian | **h.** not prose or literature |
| **d.** decimal | **i.** a method of keeping track of things |
| **e.** system | **j.** to have a reference to tenths |

## Spelling

Look, cover, write, check each word.

system ____________ ☐
library ____________ ☐
fiction ____________ ☐
specific ____________ ☐
expand ____________ ☐
different ____________ ☐
category ____________ ☐
example ____________ ☐
among ____________ ☐
decide ____________ ☐

## Word Building

"**Q**" is always followed by "**u**" except in QANTAS. From the list of '**qu**' words write each meaning.

quilt, queen, quick, quarter, quarrel, quiet, question

**a.** without a sound ____________
**b.** a monarch ____________
**c.** a bed cover ____________
**d.** half of a half ____________
**e.** very fast ____________
**f.** to row or fight ____________
**g.** enquire or examine ____________

## Sentences: Simple, Present Tense

Re-write each sentence so it is in the present tense.

**a.** She was swimming in the carnival. ____________
**b.** He was at the park. ____________
**c.** We were at the cinema. ____________
**d.** It was a good day for walking. ____________
**e.** I was at school but you were sick. ____________

## Place Value

**1.** Show each number on the abacus.

**a.** 4235

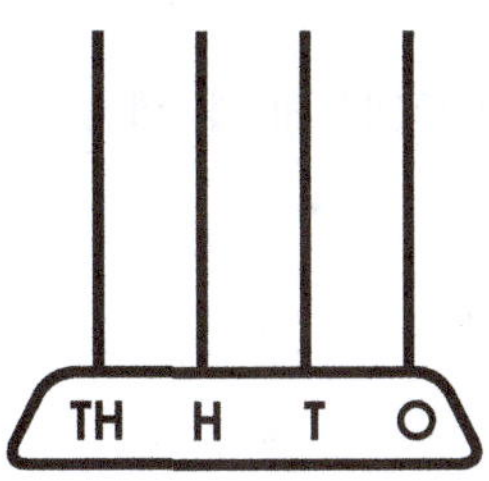


**b.** 6320

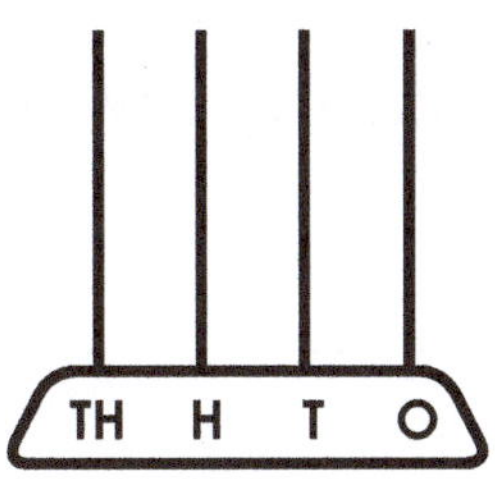


**2.** Write the number shown on each place value card.

**a.**

| TH | H | T | O |
|---|---|---|---|
| III | IIII | II | IIIII |

____________

**b.**

| TH | H | T | O |
|---|---|---|---|
| II | | IIII | II |

____________

**3.** Write 7486 in words.

____________

____________

## Multiplication and Division

**1.** Complete the multiplications and division sentences for this array.

☐ × 2 = 16 16 ÷ 2 = ☐

☐ × 8 = 16 16 ÷ 8 = ☐

**2.** Write the related multiplication and division sentence.

**a.** 27 ÷ 9 = ☐ 9 × ☐ = 27

**b.** ☐ ÷ 5 = 7 7 × 5 = ☐

**c.** 18 ÷ ☐ = 9 9 × ☐ = 18

## Should School Begin at 7.30 am and finish at 12.30 pm?

First of all I am going to put forward my reasons why I think this would be a good idea.

In Australia, the hot summer months drag on for nearly the first six to eight weeks after the summer break. This makes it very difficult for students to cope in hot classrooms during the middle of the day.

Now we start school well after the sun has risen and consequently we are learning and playing during the hottest part of the day. If we started school earlier we could avoid these hot hours and be finished our school work and go home. There we could stay inside and be cool.

On the other hand, if our parents are at work until later in the day then it would not be a good idea to be going home to an empty house. All types of problems can arise for children if they are home alone.

So, on the one hand, I think it is a good idea to start school early in the day to avoid the heat in the hottest part of the day but on the other hand to be home alone is not such a good idea.

## Understanding

Write an answer to each question.

**a.** What is the purpose of this story?

______________________________

**b.** Who should put forward the ideas in this argument?

______________________________

**c.** Why would it be better to start school early?

______________________________

**d.** What is the biggest disadvantage of starting school early?

______________________________

## Interpreting: Give your own point of view.

Write the point of view you support and why.

______________________________

______________________________

______________________________

## Language

Choose the strongest word in each sentence to strengthen your argument.

**a.** I think we (should/could) have better play equipment in the park.

**b.** When it is fine we (might/ could/ definitely will) go for the picnic.

**c.** If you (like/must), then perhaps you (should/could/would) think about it.

**d.** Why then (can/will/should/might) Tom be the school captain?

## Spelling

Look, cover, write, check each word.

forward ______ ☐
reason ______ ☐
summer ______ ☐
middle ______ ☐
during ______ ☐
finish ______ ☐
empty ______ ☐
problem ______ ☐
alone ______ ☐
idea ______ ☐

## Word Building

**"e"** is silent at the end of a word when the vowel before it says its letter name, as in **cake**. Follow the patterns to fill in the lists.

| **ate** | **like** | **home** |
|---|---|---|
| f__t__ | b__k__ | b__n__ |
| m__t__ | h__k__ | ph__n__ |
| r__t__ | s__d__ | c__n__ |
| sp__t__ | r__d__ | gn__m__ |
| gr__t__ | m__t__ | h__p__ |
| l__t__ | k__t__ | sm__k__ |

## Sentences

Use the following adjectival clauses to complete the sentences.

which was very long | that came down the street | whose bag was lost | who was my brother | whom did you say

**a.** He knew Samuel, ______.

**b.** ______ might bring those clothes inside?

**c.** Dad was very busy cutting the grass, ______.

**d.** We all went outside to look at the cars ______.

**e.** Everyone was helping the girl ______.

## The Millilitre

**1.** Write the best unit of capacity for each of these containers. (**L**) litres, (**mL**) millilitres.

**a.** 

4 ______

**b.** 
250 ______

**c.** 

200 ______

**d.** 

50 ______

**e.** 

500 ______

**2.** Write this capacity using its short form.

500 millilitres ______

## Fractions

**1.** Write an equivalent fraction.

**a.** $\frac{5}{10} =$ ___ **b.** $\frac{6}{8} =$ ___ **c.** $\frac{2}{6} =$ ___

**d.** $\frac{2}{8} =$ ___ **e.** $\frac{8}{10} =$ ___ **f.** $\frac{2}{10} =$ ___

**g.** $\frac{4}{8} =$ ___ **h.** $\frac{4}{10} =$ ___ **i.** $\frac{6}{10} =$ ___

**2.** What fraction is shaded?

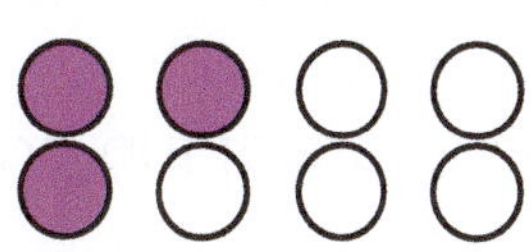

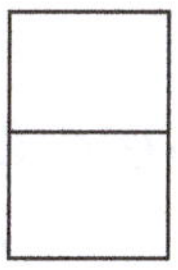

**3.** True or false?

**a.** $\frac{4}{5} = \frac{8}{10}$ ______ **b.** $\frac{3}{4} > \frac{3}{8}$ ______

**c.** $\frac{1}{4} < \frac{4}{5}$ ______ **d.** $\frac{1}{2} > \frac{4}{8}$ ______

## The Tortoise and the Hare

*(Adapted from Aesop's Fable)*

The hare always bragged about how fast he could run and finally the slow and steady tortoise had had enough. So the tortoise challenged the hare to a race.

The hare didn't have a worry about this race. After all, he was much quicker than the tortoise and he knew it. But everyone wanted to see who would win!

After starting quickly the hare looked back to see where the slow and steady tortoise was. He saw the tortoise was so far back that he decided to stop for a rest. While he rested the tortoise kept on at his slow and steady pace.

Soon the tortoise wasn't far behind the hare and he just kept walking. He never stopped until he saw the finish line.

Crowds had gathered and they cheered the tortoise which woke the hare. Hare woke and began to run but it was too late. Tortoise was over the line.

It is not good to brag about how fast you can go because slow and steady wins the race!

## Understanding

Write a sentence to answer each question.

a. What is the moral of this story?

______________________________

b. What is meant by "adapted from Aesop's Fable"?

______________________________

c. How did the hare lose this race?

______________________________

d. How did the tortoise win this race

______________________________

## Interpreting

Underline the correct words in brackets.

a. The 'he' in the 4th paragraph is (the hare / the tortoise).

b. (The hare / The tortoise) is the challenger in the race.

c. Another name given to (hare / tortoise) is (slow and ready / slow and steady).

d. A better word for 'brag' would be (skite, boast, magnify, exaggerate).

e. A fable can also be called a (fact, myth, legend).

## Language

Re-write each sentence but change all the verbs to the past tense.

a. It is raining and cold today. ______________________________

b. We are having great fun on the slide. ______________________________

c. Sam plays on his Xbox all day. ______________________________

d. Mum wears great shoes! ______________________________

e. Paris wants a new computer. ______________________________

## Spelling

Look, cover, write, check each word.

brag ______________ ☐
final ______________ ☐
challenge ______________ ☐
knew ______________ ☐
steady ______________ ☐
pace ______________ ☐
gather ______________ ☐
finish ______________ ☐
cheer ______________ ☐
woke ______________ ☐

## Word Building

Words ending in '**e**' drop the '**e**' when adding '**ing**'. Add '**ing**' to these words:

care ______ share ______
hide ______ pace ______
wake ______ rule ______
mine ______ smoke ______
time ______ strike ______
make ______ dare ______
fake ______ take ______
place ______ race ______

## Sentences

Edit the following sentences. Write the proper nouns on the line.

**a.** the statue of liberty is in new york harbour ______________
**b.** captain cook discovered the east coast of australia ______________
**c.** the capital of australia is canberra ______________
**d.** there are seven continents in the world ______________
**e.** sam and patrick are great friends ______________

## The Gram

**1.** Write grams (**g**) or kilograms (**kg**) for each item.

**a.**

300 ______

**b.**

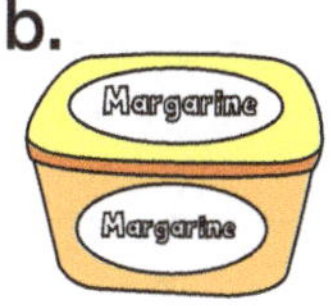


250 ______

**c.**

40 ______

**d.**

2 ______

**e.**

75 ______

**2.** Use a short form to write each mass.

**a.** 320 grams ______ **b.** 8 kilograms ______
**c.** seven hundred and fifty grams ______
**d.** 2000 grams ______

## Factors, Products and Multiples

**1.** Match the factors to its products

**a.** 2 x 7 **b.** 3 x 5 **c.** 5 x 6

15 30 12 14 40 60

**d.** 2 x 6 **e.** 10 x 6 **f.** 5 x 8

**2.** Multiply the number down the side with each number across the top.

| x | 4 | 7 | 5 | 3 | 8 | 6 | 2 |
|---|---|---|---|---|---|---|---|
| 2 | | | | | | | |
| 3 | | | | | | | |
| 5 | | | | | | | |

## Our Country Excursion

"What a wonderful day for our excursion," cried Jon. It was something the class had been looking forward to for weeks.

Houses soon disappeared, as the bus flew along the freeway out into the countryside. The surroundings had changed from inner city buildings into lush green paddocks with cows and horses and men on tractors ploughing fields.

The farmhouse was just up ahead when suddenly a herd of cows appeared on the road. In order to avoid a collision the driver had to brake hard.

"What was that awful noise?" cried Jamal.
"Was it what I think it might be?" exclaimed Jon. "Oh! Dear!"

Yes, he was right, a tyre had hit a rock when the driver swerved to miss the cows and it was now shredded. What a great start to the excursion!

## Understanding

Shade the bubble that best answers the question.

**a.** Where was the class going?
- ◯ away for the week
- ◯ to green paddocks
- ◯ on an excursion
- ◯ to the city

**b.** What changed along the way?
- ◯ homes and streets
- ◯ city buildings
- ◯ the surroundings
- ◯ cars and tractors

**c.** What was the awful noise?
- ◯ cows and horses
- ◯ the men on tractors
- ◯ a rock hitting the bus
- ◯ the tyre shredding

**d.** What did the driver do?
- ◯ braked hard
- ◯ helped the children
- ◯ avoided a collision
- ◯ got out to look around

## Interpreting

Complete each sentence.

**a.** How did the bus move? ____________________

**b.** Where was the farmhouse? ____________________

**c.** What could be seen after leaving the city? ____________________

**d.** How long had the excursion been planned? ____________________

**e.** What does '*ploughing fields*' mean? ____________________

## Language

Join the clauses in each sentence using a conjunction from the group below.

but and so because when like that unless

**a.** The class was excited ____________________ the day had arrived.

**b.** They went to town ____________________ it was time for the parade.

**c.** We can't go out ____________________ our parents tell us we can.

**d.** I went ____________________ saw the circus ____________________ it was in the park.

## Spelling

Look, cover, write, check each word.

wonderful ____________ ☐
appear ____________ ☐
disappear ____________ ☐
plough ____________ ☐
collide ____________ ☐
awful ____________ ☐
tyre ____________ ☐
brake ____________ ☐
herd ____________ ☐
swerve ____________ ☐

## Word Building

**Homophones** - words sound alike but spelt differently. Eg. herd, heard. Match each set of homophones.

| | | |
|---|---|---|
| tyre | ____________ | hoarse |
| brake | ____________ | heard |
| herd | ____________ | tire |
| there | ____________ | flu |
| horse | ____________ | weak |
| week | ____________ | their |
| flew | ____________ | break |

## Sentences: Contractions

Write each contracted word in the sentences in full.

a. He didn't know what to do when it wasn't there. ________ ________

b. They're going to have tea but he's having juice. ________ ________

c. It's too far to walk and he can't get a ride there. ________ ________

d. Let's look at this because it'll need repairing. ________ ________

e. You're too late but you'd have had to wait. ________ ________

## Grids and Locations

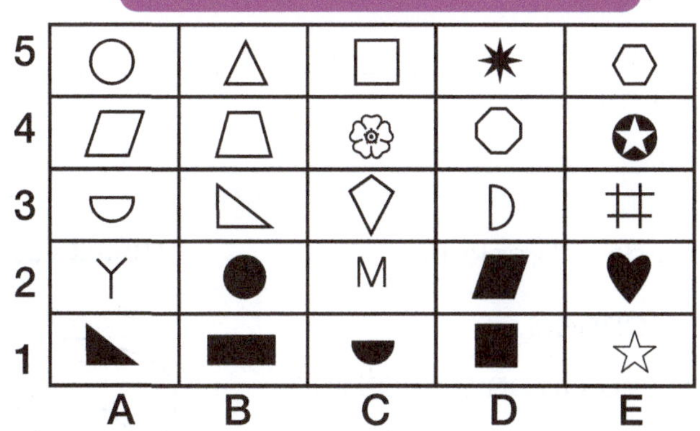


1. Draw the shapes in these positions.

a. C4 ☐ b. E2 ☐

2. Write the grid references for each of these shapes.

a. M ________ b. ✷ ________

c. ◇ ________ d. ⏢ ________

e. ◗ ________ f. ☆ ________

## Divisions

Complete each division sentence. Check repeated subtraction with your calculator.

a. $30 \div 3 =$ ☐ b. $21 \div 3 =$ ☐

c. $18 \div 2 =$ ☐ d. $35 \div 5 =$ ☐

e. $80 \div 10 =$ ☐ f. $24 \div 3 =$ ☐

g. $24 \div 2 =$ ☐ h. $51 \div 3 =$ ☐

## Money

Round off each price to the nearest 5 cents.

________ ________ ________ ________

## Reading

Use these words to fill in the spaces in each sentence.

| | | | | |
|---|---|---|---|---|
| Hello | thank you | you're welcome | please | have a nice day |
| Excuse me | good bye | May I help you? | au revoir | good morning |

**a.** It is the right thing to say ____________ when you receive a gift.

**b.** Use good manners and remember to use __________ when you ask for something.

**c.** If passing by someone or interrupting them always say ________________ .

**d.** The teacher said ____________ boys and girls, at the beginning of class.

**e.** " ________ ", said Sam. " ______________________________ ?"

**f.** French people say ________ at the end of a visit which is the same as our ________ .

**g.** It is nice to hear ______________________ in response to your thank you.

**h.** Mum said, " ________________________ " before I left for school.

## Understanding

Write an answer to each question.

**a.** Why should children be taught good manners?

______________________________________________

**b.** Who might teach manners to children?

______________________________________________

**c.** When should children begin to learn good manners?

______________________________________________

**d.** What is a good way for children to learn good manners?

______________________________________________

## Interpreting

Underline the correct word or words in brackets.

**a.** Some children need to (learn, learnt) good manners.

**b.** Always say (no please, thank you) when you are given something.

**c.** People greet each other by saying (goodbye, hello) when they meet.

**d.** It is polite to say (I beg your pardon, excuse me) when interrupting.

**e.** Remember to greet people each morning with (good afternoon, good morning).

## Language

Underline the relating verbs in each of the following sentences.

These are verbs linking pieces of information. They are not actions, speaking, thoughts or feeling verbs. They can link nouns and noun groups.

**a.** A cat is a fluffy ball of fun.

**b.** Most cars have airbags.

**c.** Your train has four carriages.

**d.** I am a boy and you are a girl.

**d.** He was a big, strong man.

**e.** We were on the couch.

## Spelling

Look, cover, write, check each word.

hello ______________________ ☐
please ______________________ ☐
welcome ______________________ ☐
excuse ______________________ ☐
thank ______________________ ☐
manner ______________________ ☐
interrupt ______________________ ☐
member ______________________ ☐
remember ______________________ ☐
response ______________________ ☐

## Word Building

Most nouns just add '**s**' to make them plural.
Add '**s**' to each of these words.

| | | | |
|---|---|---|---|
| picture | ______ | tile | ______ |
| house | ______ | cover | ______ |
| book | ______ | project | ______ |
| shoe | ______ | coat | ______ |
| tie | ______ | brick | ______ |

Write these compound words as two words.

homework ______________________

weekend ______________________

## Sentences

Use the correct verb and present participle to make each sentence correct.

**am** having **is** going **is** singing **are** running **are** talking

a. He ______________________ to town this morning , while the weather is fine.

b. They ______________________ messages to earn pocket money for holidays.

c. Because it is nearly my birthday , I ______________________ a birthday party on Sunday.

d. Everyone ______________________ in the choir at the concert this year.

e. The teacher cried, "Stop, you ______________________ too much!"

## Angles and Turns

Label each clock face rotation.

a. 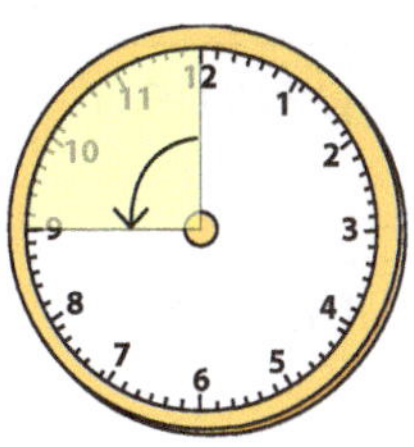

______________

b. 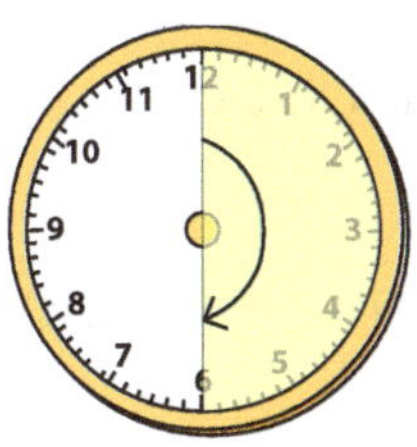

______________

c. 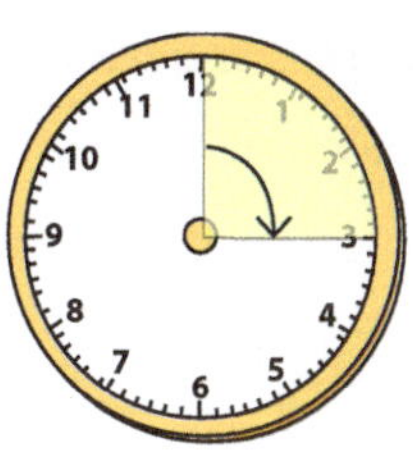

______________

d. 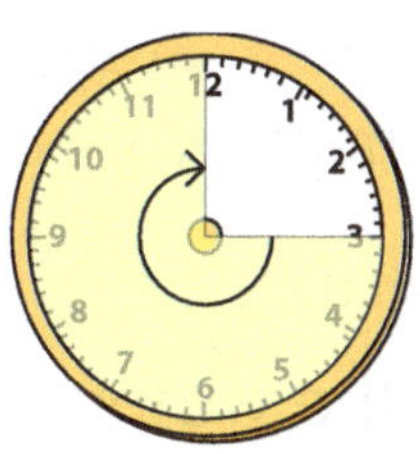

______________

## Mixed Bag

1. Write three hundred and seventy-five in numerals. ______________

2. Double 9 ______________

3. Write the missing numbers in each pattern.

   a. 216, ______ ,316, 366, ______ ,466

   b. 838, 848, ______ , ______ , 878, ______

   c. 222, 333, ______ , 555, ______ ,777

   d. 67, 82, ______ ,112, ______ , 142

4. Name each shape.

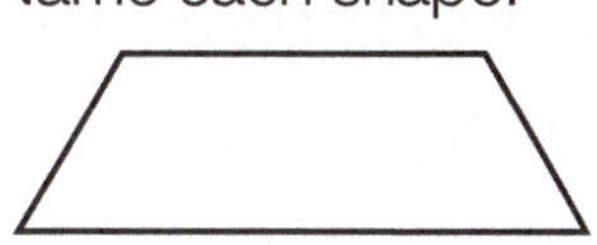

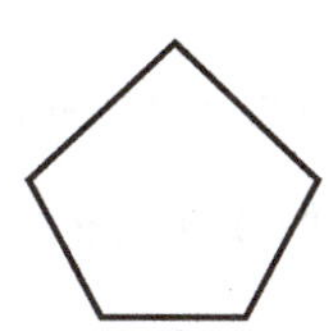

______________ ______________

## Water Displacement

**What you will need:**

A large tub filled with water
A hollow bowl with a round bottom

**What you need to do:**

Place the bowl in the tub on top of the water,
Push down on the bowl being careful not to get any water in it.
Let the dish go slowly.

**What you will find out:**

The bowl will float like a ship.
The harder you push on the bowl more water will be pushed away.
The bowl will keep floating on the water.

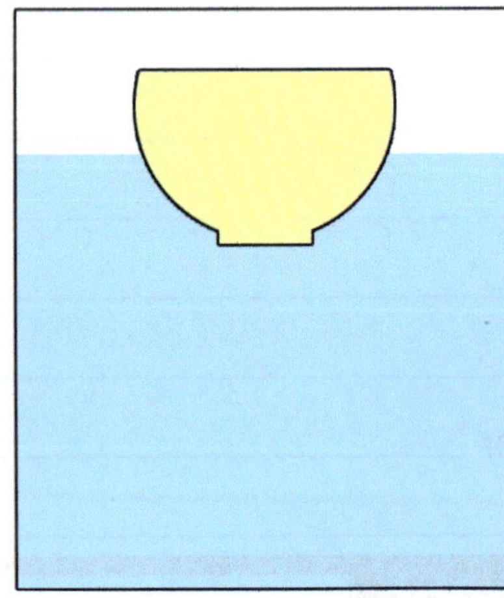

## Understanding

Circle **True** or **False** for each statement.

**a.** The bowl must have water in it to float. True False

**b.** The bowl needs to be hollow to float. True False

**c.** A hollow bowl will float on top of the water. True False

**d.** The harder the bowl is pushed into the water the better it will float. True False

**e.** The bowl is pushed by the water allowing it to float. True False

**f.** Water is displaced when the bowl is pushed into the water. True False

## Interpreting

Underline the correct word or words in brackets.

**a.** Why is it a good idea to carry out experiments?

______________________________________________

**b.** What are three main things you need to think about to conduct an experiment?

______________________________________________

**c.** Who discovered the theory of water displacement? (Look back in your book)

______________________________________________

**d.** What is the link to this experiment and a previous unit of work in this book?

______________________________________________

## Language: Verbs and Tense

Cross out the incorrect verb in each sentence.

**a.** You need a large tub (is filled / filled) with water.

**b.** Not many bowls (will floating / will float) on the water.

**c.** The bowl (are pushed / is pushed) into the water.

**d.** Water (is push / are pushed / is pushed) by (push / pushing) the bowl on the water.

# Unit 22

## Spelling

Look, cover, write, check each word.

water ______ ☐
place ______ ☐
displace ______ ☐
displacement ______ ☐
hollow ______ ☐
careful ______ ☐
helpful ______ ☐
forgetful ______ ☐
goat ______ ☐
float ______ ☐

## Word Building

When adding '**full**' to a verb drop one '**l**'.
Add '**full**' to:

hope ______ delight ______
use ______ fear ______
play ______ taste ______
hurt ______ wish ______
wonder ______ joy ______

Words ending in '**l**' double the '**l**' to add '**ed**' or '**ing**'.

travel ______ ______
marvel ______ ______
cancel ______ ______

## Sentences: Run-on Sentences

Write correctly, using good punctuation and change the words in bold.

**a.** Charles and Anna went shopping **and then** they went to the pictures.

______

**b.** The baker was making scones **and then** he was also making bread for sale.

______

**c.** Go inside **and then** watch TV **and then** have your dinner **and then** get ready for bed.

______

**d.** The rain spoilt the holiday **and then** the car broke down **and then** on the way home.

______

## Pyramids

Name each pyramid.

**a.**

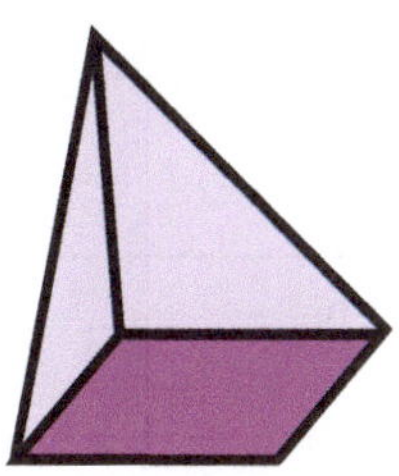

______

**b.**

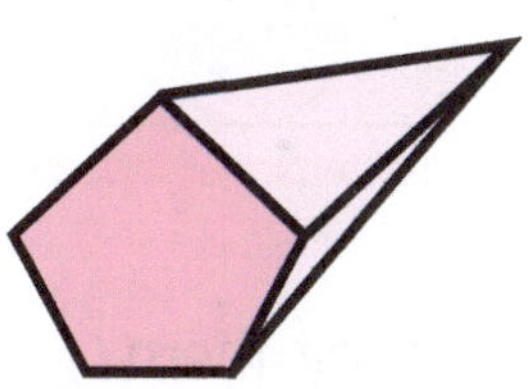

______

**c.**

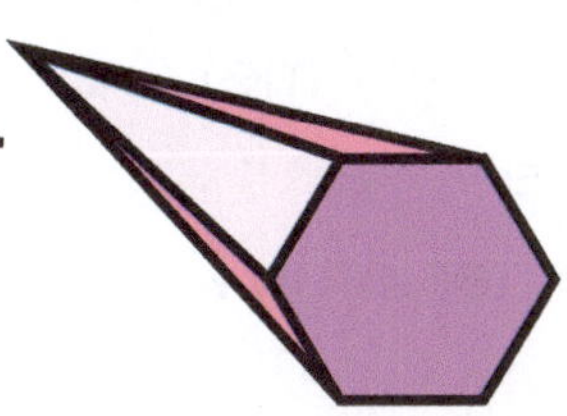

______

## Chance

**1.** If you take a letter from the box without looking, what letter are you most likely to choose?

**a.** **Most** likely to choose ______

**b.** **Least** likely to choose ______

**c.** What is the chance you are likely to pick letter **B**? ______

**d.** What fraction of the box contains letter **A**? ☐/☐

## Are there too many rules for children?

It is my opinion that adults make too many rules for children.

They have rules for getting up and going to bed. They have rules for watching TV, having meals on time, washing the dishes, cleaning the bedroom, taking out the garbage, cleaning teeth and these are just a few.

I think adults just like making rules for children. It is their way of being in charge and bossing someone around who is smaller than themselves. Why? Now don't get me wrong. I think there is a place for some rules, both at home and at school, but to have so many is just not helpful.

Children can't remember all the rules they must keep and therefore they are often break them. This is not because they want to break them but because there just too many to remember and follow. What should be done about this problem? I say make a couple of rules to begin with and when a child knows how to keep those rules begin another one and build on from there. Don't expect children to remember all the rules at once. Introduce them to rules slowly and just a few at a time. Then my opinion could change about having too many rules.

## Understanding

Write an answer to each question.

**a.** What are the reasons given for adults making rules?

______________________________

**b.** Why does the writer say adults make too many rules?

______________________________

**c.** Does the writer believe there should be rules for children? Yes or No?

______________________________

**d.** Where does the writer think there should be rules for children?

______________________________

**e.** Why are too many rules not helpful for children?

______________________________

## Interpreting

Write your response to each question.

**a.** Do you think the writer is for or against having rules for children?

______________________________

**b.** Why do you think this way?

______________________________

**c.** What would be your response to fixing this problem?

______________________________

**d.** Is the writer looking at this issue fairly? Yes or No? Explain your reason.

______________________________

**e.** Do you like having rules? Why? If not, why not?

______________________________

## Language

Circle the correct pronoun in each sentence.

Personal pronouns included: I, me, we, us, you, he, she, it, him, her, they, them.

**a.** ( I / me) went to football but ( him / he ) didn't come with ( I / me).

**b.** Do ( you / them) boys know when (him / he) will be here?

**c.** Has ( her / she) been getting mail from ( him / her ) mother lately?

**d.** Wally and ( me / I ) went to town on the bus.

# Spelling



Look, cover, write, check each word.

opinion ______________ ☐

garbage ______________ ☐

teeth ______________ ☐

children ______________ ☐

bossing ______________ ☐

couple ______________ ☐

expert ______________ ☐

introduce ______________ ☐

wrong ______________ ☐

another ______________ ☐

# Word Building

Words with silent letters at the beginning - **wrong**
Circle the silent letter in each word.

| | | | |
|---|---|---|---|
| knight | knit | knot | knew |
| gnash | thumb | lamb | knock |
| comb | gnome | write | wring |

When '**all**' is used as a prefix one '**l**' is dropped
Write each set of words as one word.

all together ______________

all most ______________ all ways ______________

all ready ______________ all so ______________

# Sentences: Pronouns for Nouns and Noun Groups

Replace the nouns or noun groups with personal pronouns in each sentence.

**a. Patrick and I** have spent all **Patrick's** money at the show.

______________________________

**b.** Ali has a dog. **Ali** walks **the dog** every day.

______________________________

**c.** The rain was heavy. **The rain** soaked into the ground and **the rain** destroyed our garden.

______________________________

**d.** This belongs to Sam. Is this one **Sam's** too?

______________________________

# Subtraction

**1.** Complete these subtractions.

**a.**

| | H | T | O |
|---|---|---|---|
| | 7 | 8 | 6 |
| - | 4 | 2 | 1 |
| | | | |

**b.**

| | H | T | O |
|---|---|---|---|
| | 8 | 3 | 5 |
| - | 6 | 2 | 1 |
| | | | |

**c.**

| | H | T | O |
|---|---|---|---|
| | 5 | 9 | 3 |
| - | 2 | 2 | 0 |
| | | | |

**2.** Regroup the ones and tens column to complete the subtraction.

**a.**

| | H | T | O |
|---|---|---|---|
| | | 5 | 13 |
| | 4 | ~~6~~ | ~~3~~ |
| - | 2 | 1 | 6 |
| | 2 | 4 | 7 |

**b.**

| | H | T | O |
|---|---|---|---|
| | | | |
| | 8 | 8 | 2 |
| - | 2 | 3 | 6 |
| | | | |

**c.**

| | H | T | O |
|---|---|---|---|
| | | | |
| | 5 | 7 | 6 |
| - | 1 | 2 | 9 |
| | | | |

# Multiplication

**1.** Write the number sentence for each continued addition.

**a.** 3+3+3+3+3+3+3= ☐

7 x 3 = ☐

**2.** Complete the web.

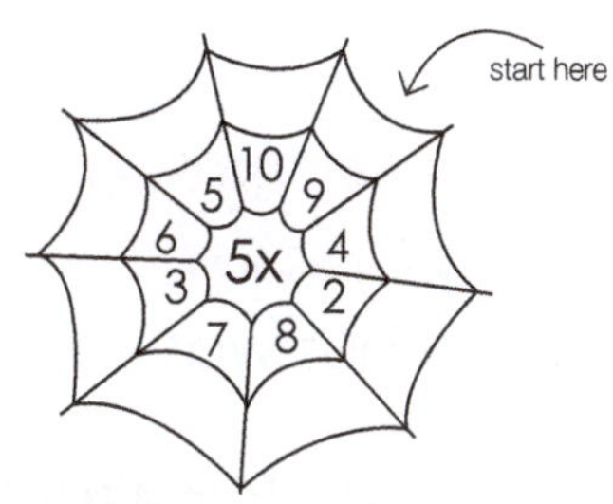


**3.** Write factors for each product.

**a.** ☐ x ☐ = 12 **b.** ☐ x ☐ = 80

Year 3 is looking for a suitable place to stay on their overnight excursion. They need to know what is available at Camp Success during June and how much it will cost per student, per night. They send the following Email to the manager of the camp.

| | |
|---|---|
| To: | campsuccess@iplay.com.au |
| Cc.. | principal@smithtown.p.s.gov.au |
| Subject: | Request for Camp Information |

Dear Camp Manager
Year 3 at Smithtown Public School would like to spend time at Camp Success this year. Could the camp accommodate 55 students on three nights from 15-17 June this year? If so, could you please send us a definite cost per student, for shared accommodation, which includes breakfast, lunch and dinner, for the duration of our stay.
Thank you on behalf of Year 3.
The Organising Committee
Smithtown Public School.
Our return Email address is: excursion@smithtown.p.s.gov.au

## Understanding

Write an answer to each question.

**a.** Where is the class hoping to stay? ______

**b.** How long will Year 3 be away? ______

**c.** What does the committee want included in the cost for a stay? ______

______

**d.** Write the school's Email address. ______

**e.** What does the 'E' in Email mean? ______

## Interpreting

Write an answer to each question.

**a.** Who will receive a copy of this Email? ______

**b.** Why is the principal receiving a copy? ______

**c.** Why is it important to ask for a cost per student? ______

______

**d.** What word tells us the students will be staying overnight?

______

## Language: Antonyms

Write an antonym (opposite meaning) to the word in italics.

**a.** The bus was very ***early***. ______

**b.** That clock is ***slow***. ______

**c.** He had the ***wrong*** answer. ______

**d.** Pat lost his ***old*** phone. ______

**e.** Please ***shut*** the window. ______

**f.** How ***cold*** is it in summer? ______

**g.** We ran home ***after*** dark. ______

**h.** ***Then*** they have no money. ______

## Spelling

Look, cover, write, check each word.

available ____________ ☐
suitable ____________ ☐
accommodate ____________ ☐
definite ____________ ☐
shared ____________ ☐
duration ____________ ☐
behalf ____________ ☐
committee ____________ ☐
request ____________ ☐
include ____________ ☐

## Word Building

Words ending in '**ie**' change '**i**' to '**y**' before adding '**ing**'. Follow the rule to complete each group.

tie ____________ die ____________

vie ____________ lie ____________

For words in the past tense just add '**d**'

tie ____________ die ____________

vie ____________ lie ____________

Form opposites of words by adding a prefix '**un**'

available ____________

suitable ____________

## Sentences

Underline the correct word in brackets to change from present to past tense.

**a.** Could you (found/find) our house without a map?
**b.** My dad (brung/bought) me some fresh cakes for tea.
**c.** Do you think he (rung/rang) to tell them where to go?
**d.** We thought we (seen/saw) who came in late.
**e.** Who was it that (done/did) all their homework last night?

## Fractions

**1.** Write the numerator and denominator for the coloured part of each shape.

**a.** 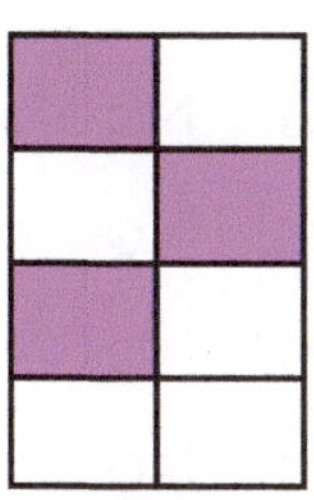 ____

**b.** 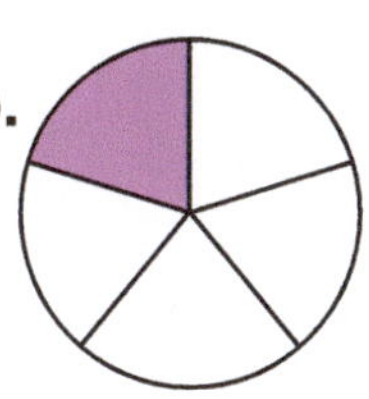 ____

**c.** 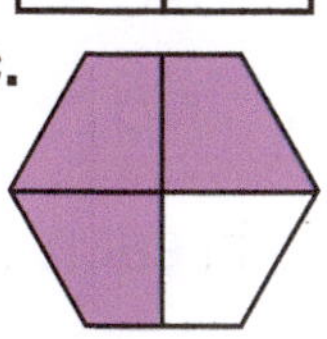 ____

**d.** 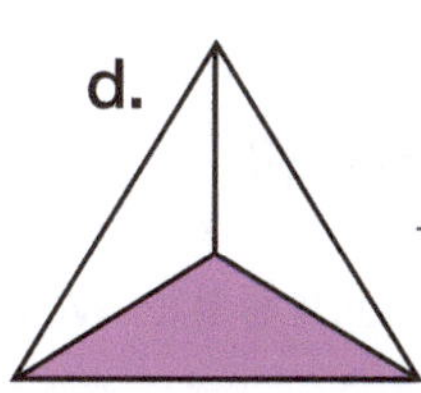 ____

**2.** Colour the given fractional part in each shape.

**a.** $\frac{3}{4}$ 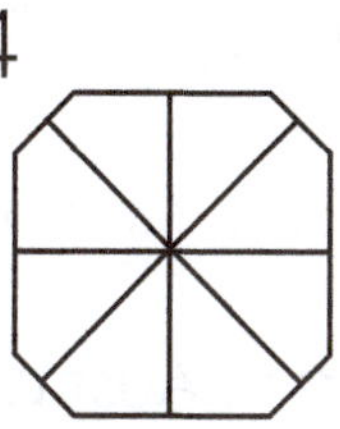

**b.** $\frac{1}{4}$ 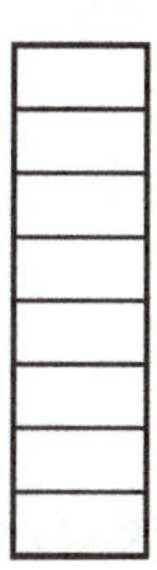

**c.** $\frac{2}{5}$ 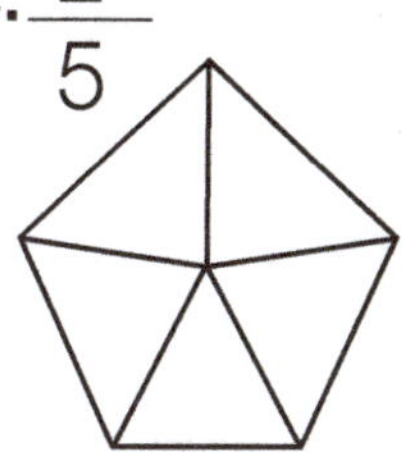

## Symmetry

**1.** Draw the other half of each object.

**a.** 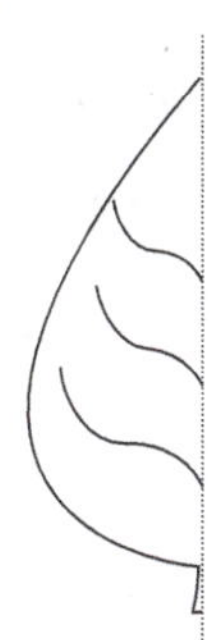

**b.** 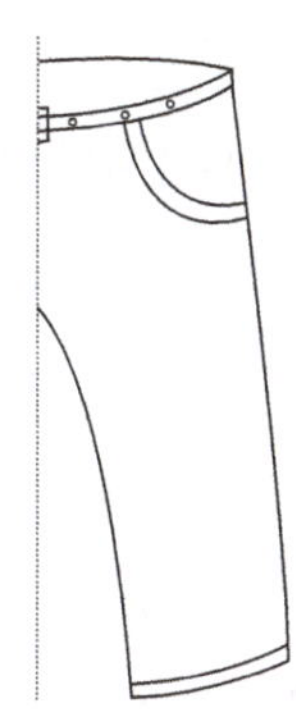

**2.** Draw the other **half** of this pattern.

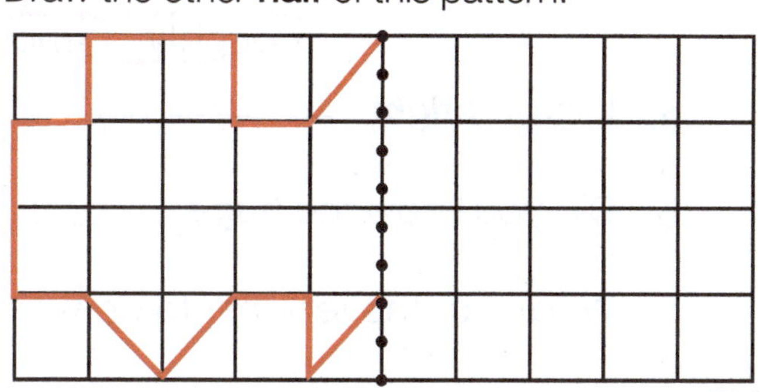

## An Acrostic Poem

Writing acrostic poetry is easy. It doesn't have to rhyme and all you need is a topic and one word relating to that topic to begin your writing. Here is an acrostic poem about the subject of Maths. Each letter of the word is written in capitals one under the other. Each line of the poem then has to be about Maths.

**M**aths add meaning to numbers
**A**rithmetic is what we do
**T**ime and measurement go together
**H**ow many or divide between
**S**ubtract and multiply can all be gleaned

Use the word MATHS to write a poem here.

M ______________________

A ______________________

T ______________________

H ______________________

S ______________________

## Understanding

Write an answer to each question.

a. Does an acrostic poem have to rhyme? ______________________

b. What are the features of an acrostic poem? ______________________

______________________

c. What is the most important element of an acrostic poem? ______________________

______________________

d. How is an acrostic poem written? ______________________

______________________

## Interpreting

Circle **Yes** or **No** to answer each question.

a. Do you like writing acrostic poems? Yes No
b. Are these poems easy to write? Yes No
c. Do you understand now how to write acrostics? Yes No
d. Do you like reading other forms of poetry? Yes No
e. Do you always understand the meaning in a poem? Yes No

## Language

Choose a better word from the list to replace the word in italics in each sentence.

naughty enormous brilliant vast

a. I saw a ***bright*** ______________ light in the night sky.

b. Did you know the ***huge*** ______________ whale beached itself?

c. What was the teacher to do with the ***bad*** ______________ child?

d. There are ***big*** ______________ areas of desert in Australia.

## Spelling

Look, cover, write, check each word.

rhyme ____________ ☐
topic ____________ ☐
relate ____________ ☐
written ____________ ☐
write ____________ ☐
between ____________ ☐
glean ____________ ☐
clean ____________ ☐
measure ____________ ☐
divide ____________ ☐

## Word Building

Match the correct **homophone** to its meaning.

piece/peace, write/right,
blew/blue, saw/sore

**a.** colour____________ **b.**correct____________
**c.** calm____________ **d.** look____________
**e.** moved____________ **f.** part____________
**g.** record____________ **h.** wound____________

Form **compound words**: stairs, time, in, down, night, ground, your, side, self, play

____________________________________

____________________________________

## Sentences: Subject/Verb Agreement

Cross out the incorrect verb in each sentence.

**a.** They ( is / are) coming to the concert with us but I (is /am) late.
**b.** Whales (swim / swims) north to warmer waters in the winter.
**c.** Our baker ( makes / make) very nice bread and cakes.
**d.** Because ( they / you ) are my sister I ( is/ am) your brother.
**e.** A good scout ( have / has ) a well-planned camping programme.

## Mixed Bag and Mentals

**1.** Write four thousand, seven hundred and forty-nine as a number.

____________________________________

**2.** Write the **even** numbers between 243 and 257.

____________________________________

**3.** Write digital time in hours and minutes.

☐ hours ☐ minutes

**4.** 5 x 9 = ☐ **5.** 10 x 6 = ☐

**6.** Write the total  = ☐

**7.** Change from $10 if you spent $7.32? ____________

## Problems

**1.** If six children had $5 each, how much would they have in total?

☐ x $ ☐ = ☐ total

**2.** Omar has two sisters and two brothers. If they each get $10 a month pocket money, how much will they get altogether?

☐ x $ ☐ = ☐ total
children

**3.** Omar also has 153 footy cards. One of his brothers has 222 cards. How many cards do they have altogether?

☐ + ☐ = ☐ footy cards

Reading

# Unit 26

## *A Formal Invitation*

An invitation is written using a mix of short sentences and points. It includes all the necessary information for the reader to want to accept it.

### My 9th Birthday Party

Dear Jo

I will be 9 on Friday.

Please come in fancy dress and help me celebrate.

**Where:** 36 Carolyn Street, Smithtown

**When:** 1 – 4 pm, Sunday, 28 October

**R.S.V.P:** 23 October

**Phone:** 6578 4397

I hope you can come.

Your friend, Carla

## Understanding

Answer each question in a full sentence.

a. Who is having a birthday party? ____________________

b. When will the party be held? ____________________

c. How old is the birthday person? ____________________

d. Where will the party be held? ____________________

e. What time will the party be on? ____________________

## Interpreting

Answer each question

a. How long will the party last? ____________________

b. What do the letters R.S.V.P mean? ____________________

c. From where do we get this term? ____________________

d. How long before the party should you reply? ____________________

e. In what way can you accept this invitation? ____________________

## Language

Time adverbs tell when (today), how long (so far) and often (frequently). Write the time adverbs in each sentence on the line.

a. It was yesterday when I was told about the new book. ____________________

b. We went often to the pictures and the theme parks. ____________________

## Spelling

Look, cover, write, check each word.

Friday ____________ ☐
Sunday ____________ ☐
Tuesday ____________ ☐
Thursday ____________ ☐
October ____________ ☐
December ____________ ☐
February ____________ ☐
April ____________ ☐
celebrate ____________ ☐
celebrations ____________ ☐

## Word Building

Words spelt with '**ph**' and have the sound of '**f**'. Match each word to its meaning.

phone, phrase, phishing, photo, graph

**a.** means of communication ____________

**b.** a snapshot ____________

**c.** part of a sentence ____________

**d.** looking for information ____________

**e.** diagram ____________

Write the missing days of the week from the spelling list.

____________

## Sentences

Re-write each sentence using the correct punctuation.

**a.** when are we going swimming I asked the teacher

____________

**b.** I think it is too cold today replied the teacher

____________

**c.** kick the ball to our best striker cried john

____________

**d.** the team all cried out go mario go

____________

## Prisms

**1.** Name each prism.

**a.**

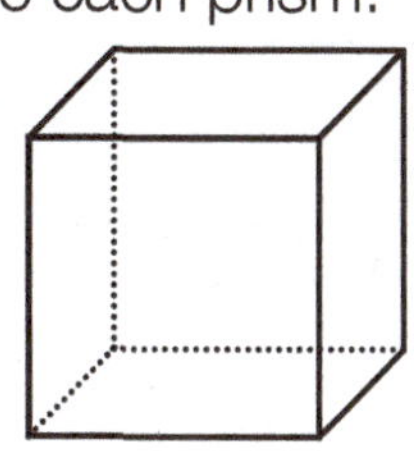

____________

**b.**

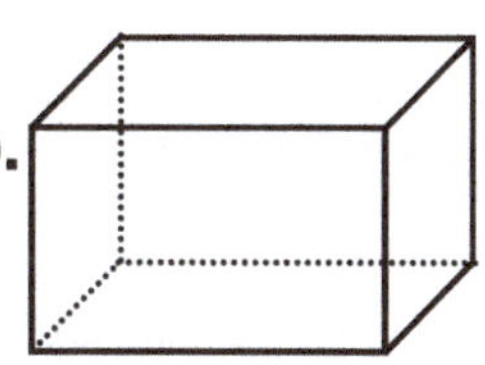

____________

____________

**c.**

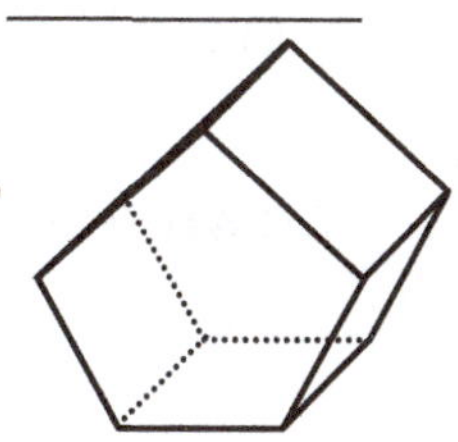

____________

____________

**d.**

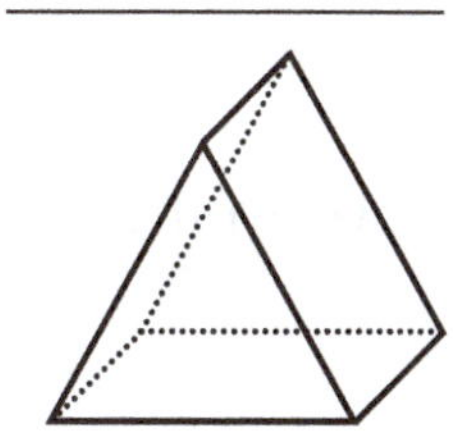

____________

____________

**2.** Fill in the facts about cubes.

| vertices | faces | edges |
|---|---|---|
| | | |

## Addition

**1.** Complete each four-digit addition.

**a.**

| | TH | H | T | O |
|---|---|---|---|---|
| | 6 | 3 | 5 | 3 |
| + | 1 | 2 | 2 | 8 |
| | | | | |

**b.**

| | TH | H | T | O |
|---|---|---|---|---|
| | 2 | 3 | 6 | 5 |
| + | 4 | 3 | 1 | 3 |
| | | | | |

**c.**

| | TH | H | T | O |
|---|---|---|---|---|
| | 4 | 1 | 6 | 2 |
| + | 3 | 5 | 2 | 2 |
| | | | | |

**d.**

| | TH | H | T | O |
|---|---|---|---|---|
| | 4 | 1 | 7 | 3 |
| + | 3 | 6 | 2 | 2 |
| | | | | |

**2.** Ali travelled 2 346 kilometres to Perth then 1 439 kilometres to Darwin. How far did he travel? Use a calculator.

☐ + ☐ = ☐

Look at this picture, discuss what is in it and your thoughts about it too.

## Understanding

Write an answer to each question.

a. What is the main idea of this picture?

______________________________

b. At what time of the year does this picture remind you?

______________________________

c. What are the children doing in this picture?

______________________________

d. What do you think about when you look at this picture?

______________________________

## Interpreting

Write an answer to each question.

a. Why do the children look so happy in the picture?

______________________________

b. Write **one** important rule you are reminded of when you look at the picture.

______________________________

c. What is the most important thing about this picture?

______________________________

d. Why do you think your idea is the most important one about the picture?

______________________________

## Language

Use one of the following adverbs or adverbial phrases correctly in each sentence.

**near** the water **under** the umbrella **beneath** the trees **down** the sand

a. The children are playing ____________________

b. One of the swimmers is sitting ____________________

c. The girl, with the surfboard, is running ____________________

d. On a warm day, people like to sit ____________________

## Spelling

Look, cover, write, check each word.

beach ______________________ □

palm ______________________ □

sunshine ______________________ □

surfboard ______________________ □

sunscreen ______________________ □

umbrella ______________________ □

swimmers ______________________ □

towel ______________________ □

dunes ______________________ □

holidays ______________________ □

## Word Building

Root Words - **AQUA** from the Latin word for Water.
More base words formed using 'aqua'.

aquatic, aquaplane, aquarium, aquamarine, aqualung

Use the correct word in each space.

The new__________centre opened today.

Divers use an ______________ to breathe.

In my ________________ there is one fish.

My pencil is an ________________ colour.

Cars often ______________ on wet roads.

## Sentences

Match the main clause with an adverbial clause to make a complex sentence.

**a.** Sam ran down the sand

**b.** He was having a great time

**c.** We are all going to town

**d.** Patrick was playing the Xbox

**e.** Mum is having visitors today

**f.** when his mates came to visit.

**g.** because it is her birthday.

**h.** before the girl could catch him.

**i.** until it began to rain.

**j.** after lunch.

## 3D Cross-Section

Draw the shape you see when the 3D object is cut along the broken line.

| | | |
|---|---|---|
| 1. | 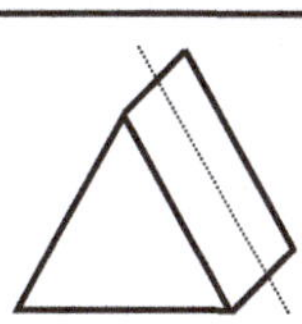 | |
| 2. | 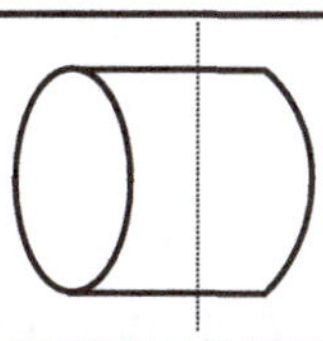 | |
| 3. | 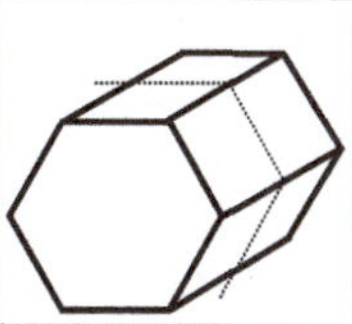 | |
| 4. | 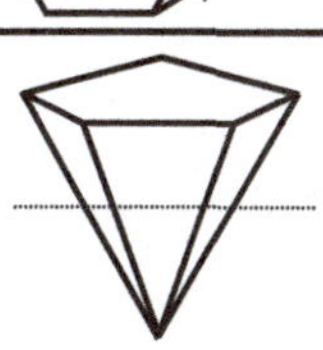 | |

## Addition

**1.** Add: **=**, **>** or **<** to make each comparison true.

**a.** $\frac{4}{10}$ □ $\frac{2}{5}$ **b.** $\frac{1}{2}$ □ $\frac{3}{5}$ **c.** $\frac{6}{10}$ □ $\frac{9}{10}$

**d.** $\frac{2}{5}$ □ $\frac{1}{4}$ **e.** $\frac{3}{5}$ □ $\frac{6}{10}$ **f.** $\frac{5}{8}$ □ $\frac{1}{2}$

**2.** Colour the given fraction for each shape.

**a.** $\frac{2}{5}$

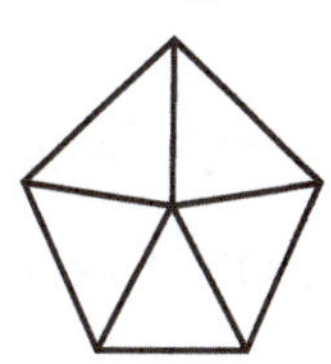

**b.** $\frac{4}{5}$

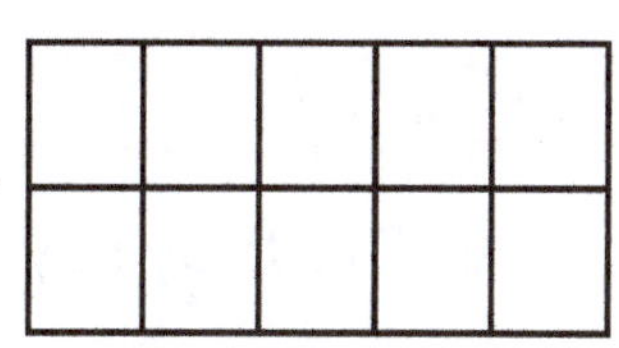

**3.** Order these fractions, **smallest** to **largest**.

$\frac{4}{10}$ $\frac{6}{10}$ $\frac{1}{10}$ $\frac{7}{10}$ $\frac{3}{10}$ $\frac{9}{10}$ $\frac{5}{10}$ $\frac{2}{10}$ $\frac{8}{10}$

___ ___ ___ ___ ___ ___ ___ ___ ___

## The First Fleet

On 13 May 1787 the ships of the First Fleet left Portsmouth, England for Australia. By July of that year they had crossed the Equator and were in the middle of the Indian Ocean by Christmas.

Captain Arthur Phillip was in charge. The fleet arrived at Botany Bay on 18 January, 1788 and then sailed on to Port Jackson, the site where the Sydney Opera House now is. It was January 26, 1788 when Arthur Phillip stepped ashore and named the place Sydney Cove.

In the fleet of eleven ships there were two naval ships, six convict ships and three ships with supplies. On the convict ships, life below decks was unbearable. The convicts were living in cramped conditions and it was hot and humid. It took nearly a year to reach our shores and about 40 of the convicts died on the way. There were 722 convicts and 17 child convicts in the fleet. Many had been convicted of petty crimes in England and for their crime their sentence was transportation, for life, to Australia.

These early settlers in Australia toiled and developed the land to feed themselves and later when they married, their families. They spread across New South Wales and used their skills to build shelters or bark huts from the timbers around them.
It was a very hard beginning for these settlers but they managed. They survived mostly on what they could find in the bush and from the help they were given by the Australian Aborigines.

## Understanding

Circle **true** or **false** for each sentence.

a. The First Fleet came from England — True False

b. We celebrate the arrival of the First Fleet every year. — True False

c. There were some child convicts on the First Fleet. — True False

d. The convicts built shelters called bark huts — True False

e. There were ten ships in the First Fleet — True False

## Interpreting

Find the meaning of each of the following words

a. transportation ____________________ b. destination ____________________

c. timbers ____________________ d. petty ____________________

e. toiled ____________________ f. shores ____________________

## Language: Relative Pronouns

Circle the correct relative pronoun in brackets in each sentence.

a. Did they say (who, whose) was going to the Opera tonight?

b. To (who, whom) were they speaking when you saw them?

c. Do you know (which, that) book is missing?

d. When we go to the football (which, whose) turn is it to buy the tickets?

e. It was this book and not (which, that) one (which, that) was missing.

## Spelling

Look, cover, write, check each word.

Equator ______________ ☐

Christmas ______________ ☐

opera ______________ ☐

Sydney ______________ ☐

supplies ______________ ☐

unbearable ______________ ☐

transport ______________ ☐

married ______________ ☐

beginning ______________ ☐

survived ______________ ☐

## Word Building

Adding **'ed'** to form words in the past tense.
Write each word in the past tense.

supply __________ marry __________

survive __________ manage __________

arrive __________ develop __________

toil __________ sail __________

cramp __________ step __________

Unjumble these words.

eadspr ______________

eganam ______________

## Sentences

State if each of the following is simple or complex. Underline the simple clause, then write the complex clause.

**a.** The bus is running late. ______________

**b.** Where is the boy who was running late for school? ______________

**c.** What will you do if you're not allowed to go today? ______________

**d.** On the Sydney Opera House there are seven sails. ______________

**e.** What day is it? ______________

## Subtraction

**1.** Find the difference.

**a.**

| | TH | H | T | O |
|---|---|---|---|---|
| | 6 | 8 | 2 | 9 |
| - | 3 | 3 | 1 | 4 |
| | | | | |

**b.**

| | TH | H | T | O |
|---|---|---|---|---|
| | 8 | 5 | 8 | 6 |
| - | 3 | 4 | 4 | 2 |
| | | | | |

**2.** Complete the subtraction webs.

**a.**

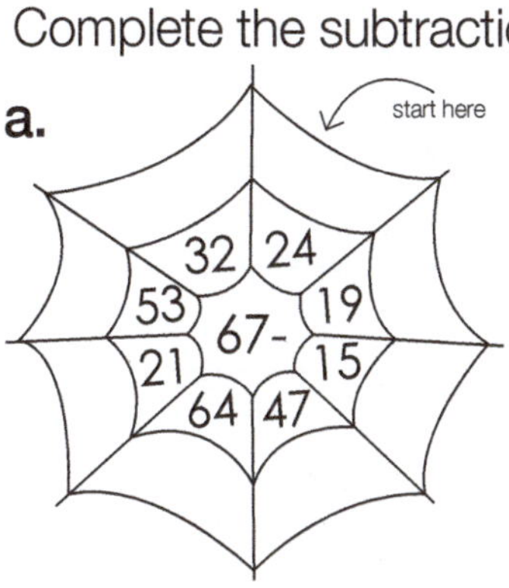


**b.**

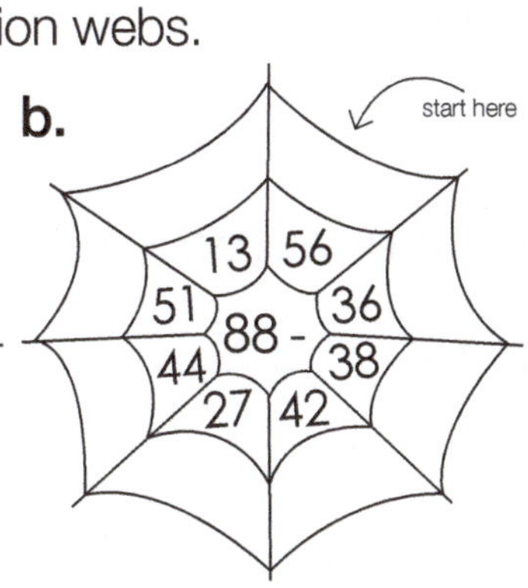


## Mass

**1.** What mass is shown on each scale.

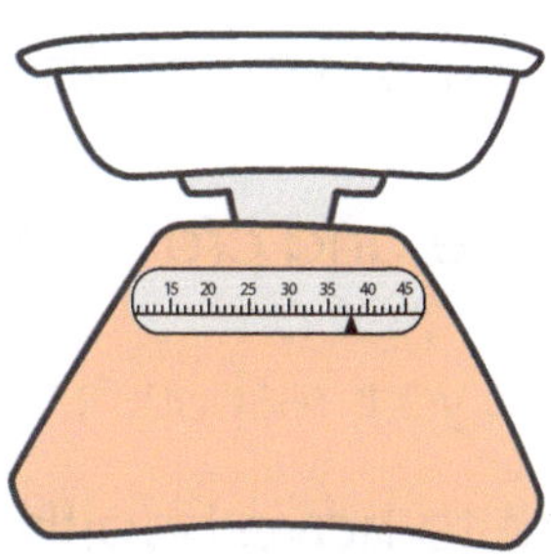

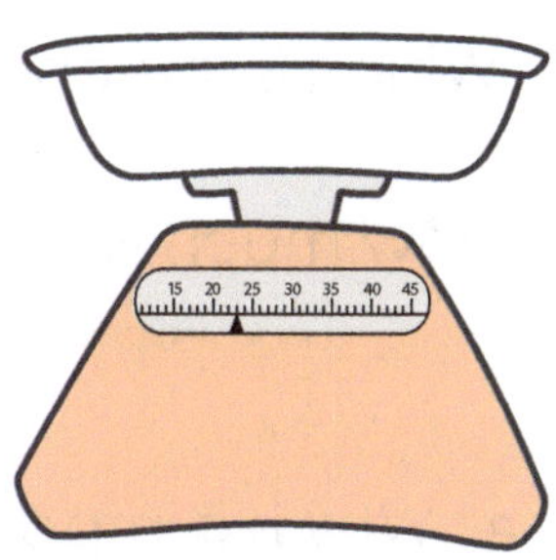

__________ __________

**2.** Write how many kilograms need to be added to the lighter arm so the scales are balanced.

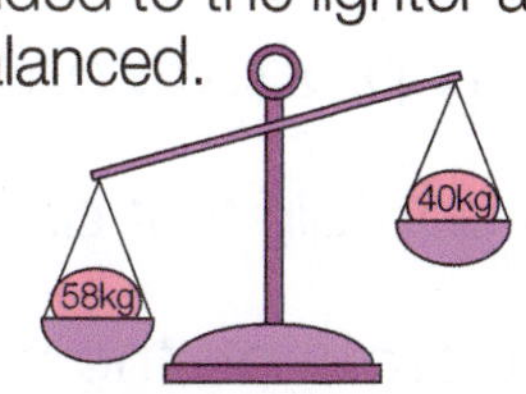


Add __________ kg

Use this advertisement to answer the questions below.

**Healthy Meals**

Salad roll + juice
$ 6.50

Carrot sticks + yoghurt
$ 3.50

fresh fruit + water
$4.00

Salad sandwich
$5.00

Cheese and Crackers
$2.50

Egg + Lettuce Sandwich
$5.00

Yoghurt
$ 1.50

Water
$ 1.00

Milk
$ 2.00

## Understanding

Write an answer to each question.

**a.** Which combination can you purchase for $4.00? ______________________

**b.** How much is the Salad roll and juice? ______________________

**c.** Which two options cost the same? ______________________

**d.** Which is the cheapest option on the menu? ______________________

**e.** How much will cheese and crackers with water cost? ______________________

## Interpreting

Write your response to each question.

**a.** Why is it important to have healthy meals?

______________________

**b.** How many product on the menu contain dairy products? ______________________

**c.** What are the dairy products on the menu? ______________________

**d.** Which products contain fruit and vegetables? ______________________

**e.** Name a carbohydrate on the menu? ______________________

# Additional Exercises Unit 30

**1.** Write whether the word in bold is used as an **adjective or adverb** in each sentence.

a. The **happy** child was **beautiful**. happy__________ beautiful__________

b. The **large** fish had **big** bones. large __________ big __________

c. **Many** people came to town **today**. many __________ today __________

**2. Demonstrative Adjectives** can be singular (this or that) or plural (these or those). Circle the correct adjective in each sentence.

a. Who owns (this, these) shoes?

b. Where does (these, this) book belong?

c. On and off (these, that) dog barks.

d. How far will (that, these) rope reach?

**3. Change the gender** of the noun or pronoun in each sentence.

a. He was running late for school and his mother was late for work.

b. My grandfather is very ill so he has to be in hospital until he is well.

c. There were twenty girls and five boys in the class and a male teacher.

**4. Punctuate** each sentence correctly.

a. mr and mrs shoesmith were able to find doctor fren for jon

________________________________________

b. when the lion king was in sydney i couldnt wait to see it

________________________________________

c. the parliament of australia is in canberra

________________________________________

## Multiplication

**1.** Write the number sentence for each array.

a.

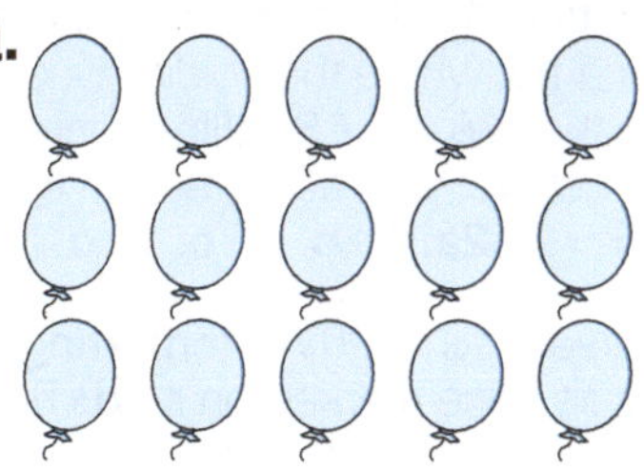

☐ x ☐ = ☐

b.

☐ x ☐ = ☐

**2.** Complete these simple multiplications.

a. 8 ×2 ___

b. 6 ×3 ___

c. 7 ×5 ___

d. 4 ×5 ___

e. 7 ×2 ___

f. 8 ×5 ___

g. 9 ×2 ___

h. 8 ×3 ___

## Multiplies and Factors

**1.** Circle the **prime** numbers.

1 2 3 4 5 6 7

8 9 10 11 12 13 17

**2.** Colour the multiples of the centre number.

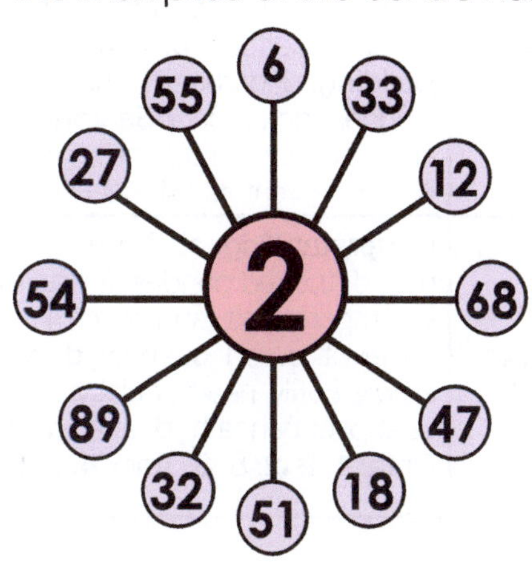

# Answers

| | |
|---|---|
| **Unit 1** | **Understanding: a** To begin before the traffic built up **b.** in the back seat **c.** annually **d.** the tents **e.** two hours **/ Interpreting: a.** false **b.** false **c.** true **d.** false **e.** true **/ Language: 1.** Josie and I **/** cornflakes and toast / we **/ 2.** Dad would need to hire tents at the campsite. **OR** Dad would need to buy new ones. **OR** Dad would have to go back home! **/ Spelling:** Parent **/ Word Building:** packed, pulled, founded. Slapped, robbed, skipped, stopped, patted. **/ Sentences: a.** tents **b.** Josie **c.** mum, tents **d.** dad **/ The Centimetre: 1a.** 30 cm **b.** 10 cm **c.** 5 cm **/ 2.** 21 cm **/ Time to the Quarter Hour: a.** matches **h; b** matches **g; c** matches **f; d** matches **e;** |
| **Unit 2** | **Understanding:** tick - a,b.c.d. not e. **/ Interpreting: a.** Internet **b.** Search Engine **c.** Email **d.** World Wide Web **/ Language: a.** key **b.** search **c.** Email **d.** business **e.** personal **f.** electronic **/ 2.** When I use the Internet I need to spell correctly if I want to find out information. **/ Spelling:** Parent **/ Word Building:** piece, niece, chief, thief, believe, brief. **/ Circle:** saw, het, ship, four, sum FOR was, the, shop, for, some **/ Sentences: a** matches **h**; **c** matches **f**; **e** matches **j**; **g** matches **b**; **i** matches **d**. **/ Place Value: 1a.** 3,426 **b.** 1, 376; **2a.** 3 ones **b.** 6 hundreds **/ Number Facts: 1. b.** 5, **c.** 5 **2a.** 5 **b.** 1 **c.** 3 **a.** 15 **b.** 18 **c.** 14 **d.** 16 **e.** 13 **f.** 15 |
| **Unit 3** | **Understanding: a.** 3 **b.** 3 **c.** 2 **d.** 4 **/ Interpreting: a.** 1 year **b.** Westminster Abbey **c.** 86 **d.** parent **/ Language: a.** were **b.** was **c.** attended **d.** celebrated **/ Spelling:** Parent **/ Word Building:** sitting, rubbing, jetting, stepping, skipping, dropping, chopping, slapping **/ Sentences: a.** Subject: The princess Verb: was **b.** Subject: The king Verb: died **c.** Subject: We Verb: celebrated **d.** Subject: I verb: thought **/ Money: a.** 2 lots of $2, 20c, 10c, 5c. **b.** $2, $1, 50c, 20c, 5c **/ Chance:** parent |
| **Unit 4** | **Understanding: a.**ii **b.**iii **c.**iii **d.** ii **e.**iii **/ Interpreting: a.** $40 **b.** yes **c.** before lunch **d.** no **Language: 1.** Downtown Zoo **2 a.** Downtown Zoo **b.** proper **/ Spelling:** Parent **/ Word Building:** happiness, prettiness, funniness, silliness, naughtiness/ crying, trying, buying, saying, enjoying. **/ Sentences: a.** circle is, underline standing **b.** circle are, underline going **c.** circle am, underline looking **d.** circle were, underline getting **e.** circle was, underline having **/ Number Patterns: 1a.** 500 **b.** 1775 **2a.** 8368 - 8370 **b.** 6999 - 7001 **3.** 3915, 5628, 8314, 8316, 9742 **/ Fractions: 1a.** colour 3 parts, **1b.** colour one part **2.** Colour 4 balloons, colour 3 cupcakes |
| **Unit 5** | **Understanding: a.** yes **b.** yes **c.** yes **d.** no **e.** yes **/ Interpreting: a.** 3, **b.** 4, **c.** 4, **d.** 1 **/ Language: a.** salad **b.** each, small **c.** fresh **d.** small **/ Spelling:** Parent **/ Word Building:** cow, how, now, proud, plough, bough, crown, drown, howl. / Parent **Sentences: a.** We went to town. **b.** Mum and I had lunch **c.** We caught the bus home **d.** Do you know **e.** There will be no rain. **Capacity: 1.** 250 mL **2.** 6L **3.** 60L **4.** 300mL **5.** 5L **6.** 100mL **/ Symmetry:** Parent |
| **Unit 6** | **Understanding: a.** How to make a 'phone call **b.** All the credit will be used **c.** important news **d.** Store them in the 'phone **e.** Do the same as others do and follow the fashion. **/ Interpreting: a.** no **b.** yes **c.** yes **d.** parent **e.** parent **/ Language: 1a.** follow **b.** call **c.** push **d.** use **2** swung, raced, ran, called, arrived **/ Spelling:** Parent **/ Word Building:** friends, number, family, might, remember. when ever, may be **/ Sentences: a.** My phone is blue and it is an iPhone. **b.** I need more credit but I have to save some money first. **c.** We were having a picnic but we left too late. **/ Vertical Addition: 1a.** 869 **b.** 879 **c.** 4968 **d.** 9599 **2.** $478. **/ Angles:** colour **b. e.** tick **a. f.** |
| **Unit 7** | **Understanding:** parent. **/ Interpreting: a.** Mr Bert New **b.** In the Main Street of Smithtown **c.** A grocery shop **d.** food **e.** 2008 **/ Language: a.** main (a) **b.** windows (n) **c.** yellow and blue (a) **d.** entrance (a) **e.** big, bold (a) **f.** tall, black (a) **/ Spelling:** Parent **/ Word Building:** wide, happy, winter, last, after, end, white, old **/ Sentences: a.** Our shoes are red, black, blue and brown. **b.** Was there a bright yellow, round ball on the field? **c.** The colours of the rainbow are red, orange, yellow, green, blue, indigo and violet. **Vertical Subtration: 1a.** 361 **b.** 324 **c.** 534 **d.** 362 **2.** 184 – 122 = 62 **/ Location: 1.** Orange juice **2.** Biscuits |
| **Unit 8** | **Understanding: 1.** it gives joy to its owner **2.** They keep them safe **/ Interpreting: 1a.** fend off snakes; **b.** keep children warm if lost; **2.** a great friend and helper **3.** its owner **4.** a soldier's camp; where the soldier lives **/ Language: a.** He stayed in bed. **b.** She bought a show bag. **c.** They are on the swings. **/ Spelling:** parent **/ Word Building:** parent check **/ Sentences: a.** because **b.** could, if **c.** I firmly believe, you will agree **d.** I think, should. **Tables: 1a.** 9 **b.** 9 **c.** 7 **d.** 7 **/ Multiplication: 1a.** 5 x 5 = 25 **1b.** 4 x 5 = 20 **2a.** 10 **b.** 45 **c.** 15 **d.** 30 |
| **Unit 9** | **Understanding: 1a.** an egg sandwich **2.** the works hamburger **3.** tea or coffee **4.** $11.00 **/ Interpreting: a.** in outback Australia **b.** That's where you find Roadhouses **c.** Each drink has its price marked on it. **d.** The Roadhouse is very isolated and cannot get stock easily. **/ Language: a.** fish and chips, dollars **b.** cheese, vegemite, lettuce **c.** works hamburger **d.** cup tea or coffee; dollars **e.** eggs, drink **/ Spelling:** Parent **/ Word Building:** underneath, underground, underline, understood, birthday, Sunday, weekday, everyday, tomatoes, dingoes, potatoes. **/ Sentences: a.** "Bring me back an egg and lettuce sandwich please." **b.** "These fish and chips are hot," cried Josie. **c.** "I just love these bacon and eggs," said dad. **Division: 1.** 18 ÷ 3 = 6 **2.** 10 **3.** 8 **4.** 9 **5.** Parent **6.** 24 ÷ 3 = 8 |
| **Unit 10** | **Understanding: a.** The emu **b.** swinging from rope to rope **c.** They came right up and looked me in the eye **d.** the red pandas. It was too hot **e.** 2 weeks **/ Interpreting: a.** a safe place **b.** at risk of being hurt **c.** in temperatures ranging from - 40 to + 40 degrees **d.** In Australia **e.** 22-23 hours each day. **/ Language: a.** eucalypt **b.** red **c.** snow **d.** eastern grey **e.** black-handed spider **/ Spelling:** parent **/ Word Building:** quickly, slowly, softly, nearly, quietly, really, beautifully, importantly, finally **/ Sentences: a.** yesterday, out **b.** beautifully, on **c.** above, beneath **d.** after, away, time **e.** before, into.<br>**Data: 1.** 9 **2.** 8 **3.** Train **4.** 3 **5.** 6 **6.** 3 **7.** 30 |

# Answers

| | |
|---|---|
| **Unit 11** | **Understanding: a.** To show how to pronounce it. **b.** two years **c.** Washington, DC **d.** 2001 **e.** one / **Interpreting: a.** reinforced concrete, outer walls **b.** can be found there **c.** for the Department of Defense in America **d.** is on the other side of the river / **Language: a.** intelligence **b.** headquarters **c.** hijack **d.** architect **e.** pentagon / **Spelling:** Parent / **Word Building:** handful, useful, mindful, careful, hopeful, truthful, shameful / **Sentences: a.** Mr Spring and Mrs Summer. **b.** The Department of Defense is in America. Note how America spells defense. **c.** In Australia, we have a governor general who represents Queen Elizabeth. / **Money and Change: a.** $3.75 **b.** $2.90 **c.** Two dollars and seventy five cents. / **Division and Multiplication: 1. a.** 4 **b.** 8 **c.** 8 **d.** 7 **e.** 9 **f.** 6 **2. a.** 21 **b.** 16 **c.** 30 **d.** 45 **e.** 60 **f.** 33 |
| **Unit 12** | **Understanding:** correct order: **b, e, c, d, a** / **Interpreting: a.** help **b.** the same help **c.** supply or give, **d.** up-to-date **e.** to get **f.** depend **g.** sure **h.** science and engineering / **Language:** I believed it was important; should; If; can and should; Don't you agree? **2.** Parent / **Spelling:** Parent / **Word Building:** parent check / **Sentences: a.** on Tuesday **b.** before dark **c.** after lunch **d.** every day **e.** through the bush **Angles: a.** acute **b.** right **c.** obtuse **d.** acute **e.** reflex **f.** obtuse / **Time to the Minute: 1.a.** 6:44 **b.** 10:20 **2.** Match **a-f , b-d, c-e** |
| **Unit 13** | **Understanding:** Order - **3/**1770 **1/**1788 **4/**1851 **5/**1901 **2/**1914 **6/**1945 / **Interpreting: a.** yes **b.** no **c.** yes **d.** yes **e.** yes **Interpreting: a.** Captain Cook's ship **b.**The ships that first came together to Australia in 1788 **c.** In Victoria near Ballarat **d.** He was an explorer, from Great Britain. / **Language: a.** circle - in. underline-happily **b.** circle - towards, underline - slowly **c.** circle - for, underline - excitement **d.** circle - at, underline - inside **Spelling:** Parent / **Word Building:** parent check / **Sentences: a.** because **b.** so **c.** since **d.** so that / **Vertical Subtraction: 1a.** 543 - 22 = 521 **b.** 457 - 135 = 322 **2.** 642 / **Chance:** colour **a.** |
| **Unit 14** | **Understanding: a.** true **b.** false **c.** true **d.** false **e.** true / **Interpreting: a.** iron **b.** sail **c.** empty **d.** move away **e.** mass **f.** very old. / **Language: a.** circle - water, underline - the ship afloat **b.** circle - ship, underline - pushes the water **c.** circle - ships, underline - in shipyards around the World **d.** circle - sailors, underline - in every Australian port **e.** circle - hours, underline - the big ships glide into port **f.** circle - Archimedes, underline - an ancient Greek, the principle of water displacement. / **Spelling:** Parent / **Word Building:** parent / **Sentences:** order: **d, b, e, c, a** / **Numbers to 10 000: 1a.** 4 863 **b.** 8 765 **c.** 4 982 **d.** 5 634 **2a.** 4 675 **b.** 6 268 **c.** 8 999 / **The Kilogram: a.** 70g **b.** 6 kg **c.** 3 kg **d.** 700g **e.** 850g **f.** 3 kg |
| **Unit 15** | **Understanding:** tick **b, c, g, i, j** / **Interpreting: a.** To thank Sam for his birthday present. **b.** He has had fun doing a few experiments. He will ask his teacher to do some with the class. To ask Sam what he would like for his birthday. **c.** For Sam to write in time to let him know what he wants for a present. / **Language: a.** mine **b.** hers **c.** yours **d.** his **e.** theirs **e.** ours / **Spelling:** Parent / **Word Building:** scissors, pliers, trousers, glasses, slacks, would wood. / **Sentences: a.** whispered **b.** asked **c.** called **d.** tell **e.** answered / **Length: 1.a.**30cm **b.**4m **c.**2m **d.**21 cm **2.** Parent / **Fractions: 1a.** colour 2 balloons **b.** colour 2 apples **2.a.**2/5 **b.**2/3 **c.**3/8 **d.** ½ |
| **Unit 16** | **Understanding: a.** To tell the reader something is going to happen. **b.** south **c.** it was the cheapest way to travel. **d .** boys. Because it is about a boy. / **Interpreting: a.** 3 **b.** 2 **c.** 1 **d.** 3 / **Language: a.** the, a **b.** an, an, a **c.** a, a. / **Spelling:** Parent / **Word Building:** tomatoes, potatoes, echoes, dingoes, heroes, volcanoes, avocados / **Sentences: a.** Underline - Run fast. Write: because it is raining. **b.** Underline - Go to the letterbox. Write - before you wash **c.** Underline - Undo the lock, Write - then walk inside. **d.** Underline - Repair your shoes. Write - while you can. **e.** Underline - You can do it easily - write - knowing how / **Subtraction: 1.a.** 56 **b.** 38 **c.** 27 **2.** Clockwise = 57, 31, 5, 52, 38, 26, 19, 40 / **Width and Height: 1.** 15cm wide 13cm high **2.** 5cm long 3cm high **3.** 16cm |
| **Unit 17** | **Understanding: a.** It is named after the person who invented the system. **b.** The librarian **c.** numbers and decimals **c.** In the 300s section at 388.3 / **Interpreting: a.** 690 **b.** 780 **c.** 400 **d.** 220 **e.** 370 **f.** 950 / **Language:** match **a - g, b - h, c - f, d - j, e - i** / **Spelling:** Parent / **Word Building: a.** quiet **b.** queen **c.** quilt **d.** quarter **e.** quick **f.** quarrel **g.** question / **Sentences: a.** She is swimming in the carnival **b.** He is at the park **c.** We are at the cinema **d.** It is a good day for walking **e.** I am at school but you are sick. / **Place Value: 1.a.** 4235 **b.** 6320 **2a.** 3 425 **b.** 2 042 **3.** Seven thousand, four hundred and eighty six. / **Multiplication and Division: 1.** 8, 8 and 2, 2. **2a.** 3, 3 **b.** 35, 35 **c.** 2, 2 |
| **Unit 18** | **Understanding: a.** To argue a point of view **b.** parents or the school council **c.** to beat the heat; to work better; **d.** parents might not be at home at 12:30pm if they work and children would be home alone, which could be dangerous. / **Interpreting:** Parent / **Language: a.** should **b.** definitely will **c.** must, should **d.** should / **Spelling:** Parent / **Word Building:** Parent check / **Sentences: a.** who was my brother **b.** whom did you say **c.** which was very long **d.** that came down the street e. whose bag was lost. / **The Millilitre: 1a.** 4 L **b.** 250 mL **c.** 200 mL **d.** 50 mL **e.** 500 mL **2.** 500 mL / **Fractions: 1a.** ½ **b.** ¾ **c.** 1/3 **d.** ¼ **e.** 4/5 **f.** 1/5 **g.** ½ **h.** 2/5 **i.** 3/5 **2.** 3/8 **3a.** true **b.** true **c.** true **d.** false |
| **Unit 19** | **Understanding: a.** The fastest to do things does not always win. **b.** Aesop wrote the fable but the reading is not as he wrote it. It is an interpretation of the fable. **c.** He was too sure of himself and he went to sleep because he thought he would always be faster than the tortoise. **d.** The tortoise just kept on going until he finished and did not stop like the hare. / **Interpreting: a.** the tortoise **b.** The hare **c.** tortoise / slow and steady **d.** boast **e.** myth. / **Language: a.** It was raining … **b.** We were having **c.** Sam played **d.** Mum wore **e.** Paris wanted / **Spelling:** Parent / **Word Building**: parent check / **Sentences: a.** The Statue of Liberty, New York **b.** Captain Cook, Australia **c.** The, Australia, Canberra **d.** There, World **e.** Sam and Patrick / **The Gram: 1a.** 300g **b.** 250g **c.** 40 kg **d.** 2 kg **e.** 75g **2a.** 320g **b.** 8kg **c.** 750g **d.** 2kg / **Factors, Products and Multiples: 1a.**14 **b.**15 **c.**30 **d.**12 **e.**60 **f.**40 **2.** 8,14,10,6,16,12,4/12,21,15,9,24,18,6/20,35,25,15,40,30,10 |

# Answers

| | |
|---|---|
| **Unit 20** | **Understanding:** shade **a-3, b-3, c-4, d-3 / Interpreting: a.** it flew along the freeway **b.** in the country **c.** lush green paddocks with cows and horses and men on tractors ploughing fields **d.** weeks **e.** turning over the soil for planting **/ Language: a.** because **b.** when **c.** unless **d.** and, when **/ Spelling:** Parent **/ Word Building:** tyre - tire; brake - break; herd - heard; there - their; horse - hoarse; week - weak; flew - flu **/ Sentences: a.** did not, was not **b.** they are, he is c. it is, can not **d.** let us, it will **e.** you are, you would **/ Grids and Locations: 1a.** flower **b.** heart **2a.** C2 **b.** D5 **c.** C3 **d.** B4 **e.** C1 **f.** E1 **/ Division: a.** 10 **b.** 7 **c.** 9 **d.** 7 **e.** 8 **f.** 8 **g.** 12 **h.** 17 **/ Money: a.** \$3.25 **b.** \$2.20 **c.** \$1.00 **d.** \$2.80 |
| **Unit 21** | **Responses: a.** thank you **b.** please **c.** excuse me **d.** good morning **e.** Hello, May I help you? **f.** au revoir, good bye **g.** you're welcome **h.** have a nice day **/ Understanding: a.** to show people politeness **b.** parents, grandparents and teachers as well as older brothers and sisters **c.** as soon as possible, when they begin to understand and talk **d.** by adults showing through example **/ Interpreting: a.** learn **b.** thank you **c.** hello **d.** excuse me **e.** good morning **/ Language: a.** is **b.** have **c.** has **d.** am, are **e.** was **f.** were **/ Spelling:** Parent **/Word Building:** parent check/ home work, week end **/ Sentences: a.** is going **b.** are running **c.** am having d. is singing **e.** are talking **/ Angles and Turns: a.** a quarter turn anti-clockwise **b.** half turn clockwise **c.** a quarter turn clockwise **d.** three quarter turn clockwise **/ Mixed Bag: 1.** 375 **2.** 18 **3.a.** 266, 416 **b.** 858, 868, 888 **c.** 444, 666 **d.** 97, 127 **4.** Trapezium, pentagon |
| **Unit 22** | **Understanding: a.** false **b.** true **c.** true **d.** false **e.** true **f.** true **/ Interpreting: a.** To best learn how things happen **b.** What you will need, what you need to do and what you found out **c.** Archimedes **d.** it is about the same thing - water displacement **/ Language: a.** filled **b.** will float **c.** is pushed **d.** is pushed, pushing **/ Spelling:** Parent **/ Word Building:** parent check **/ Sentences: a.** then **b.** and **c.** and, then, and **d.** and, delete and then **/ Pyramids: a.** square pyramid **b.** pentagonal pyramid **c.** hexagonal pyramid **/ Chance: 1a.** A **b.** D **c.** 1 in 4 **d.** ½ |
| **Unit 23** | **Understanding: a.** they like making them, they like being in charge and bossing someone smaller than they are **b.** because they don't like having too many **c.** yes **d.** at home and at school **e.** it is hard to remember all of them **/ Interpreting: a.** neither for or against **b.** because there are both sides to the argument in the reading **c.** parent **d.** yes. The writer has given reasons for and against having too many rules. **e.** parent **/ Language: a.** I, he, me **b.** you, he **c.** she, her **d.** I **/ Spelling:** Parent **/ Word Building:** parent check. **/ Sentences: a.** We … his money **b.** She walks it … **c.** It soaked … it destroyed **d.** his **/ Subtraction: 1a.** 365 **b.** 214 **c.** 373 **2. b.** 646 **c.** 447 **/ Multiplication: 1a.** 21, 7 x 3 = 21 **2.** clockwise: 45, 20, 10, 40, 35, 15, 30, 25, 50 **3a.** 4x3 or 6x2 or 12x1 **b.** 8x10 or 5x16 or 80x1 or 20x4 or 40x2 |
| **Unit 24** | **Understanding: a.** At Camp Success **b.** three days **c.** shared accommodation and breakfast, lunch and dinner **d.** excursion@smithtown.p.s.gov.au **e.** Electronic **/ Interpreting: a.** The principal **b.** So he/she knows what the class is doing **c.** To let the parents know how much to pay for a child **d.** overnight accomodation **/ Language:** a. late **b.** fast **c.** right **d.** new **e.** open **f.** hot **g.** before **h.** now **/ Spelling:** Parent **/ Word Building:** parent check **Sentences: a.** find **b.** bought **c.** rang **d.** saw **e.** did **/ Fractions: 1a.** 3/8 **b.** 1/5 **c.** ¾ **d.** 1/3 **2a.** colour 6 parts **b.** colour 2 parts **c.** colour 2 parts **/ Symmetry: 1a. b.** and **c.** parent check |
| **Unit 25** | **Understanding: a.** no **b.** it needs a topic and one word relating to the topic. **c.** each line has to be about the chosen topic **d.** with the topic word spelt out and the first letter written in capitals at the beginning of each line. **/ Interpreting: a. b. c. d. e.** parent **/ Language: a.** brilliant **b.** enormous **c.** naughty **d.** vast **/ Spelling:** Parent **/ Word Building: a.** blue **b.** right **c.** peace **d.** saw **e.** blew **f.** piece **g.** write **h.** sore **/ Compound Words:** downstairs, playground, nightime, inside, yourself **/ Sentences: a.** are, am **b.** swim **c.** makes **d.** you, am **e.** has **/ Mixed Bag: 1.** 4 749 **2.** 244, 246, 248, 250, 252, 254, 256 **3.** 4 hours 53 minutes **4.** 45 **5.** 60 **6.** 17 **7.** \$2.68 **/ Problems: 1.** 6 x 5 = \$30 **2.** 5 x 10 = \$50 **3.** 153 + 222 = 375 |
| **Unit 26** | **Understanding: a.** Carla **b.** On Sunday, 28 October **c.** 9 **d.** 36 Carolyn Street, Smithtown **e.** between 1 - 4 pm **Interpreting: a.** 3 hours **b.** Reply if you please **c.** From the French **d.** 4 days before the party **e.** By telephone **Language: a.** yesterday, when **b.** often **/ Spelling:** Parent **/ Word Building: a.** phone **b.** photo **c.** phrase **d.** phishing **e.** graph / Saturday, Monday, Wednesday **/ Sentences: a.** When are we going swimming?" I asked the teacher. **b.** "I think it is too cold today," replied the teacher. **c.** "Kick the ball to our best striker," cried John. **d.** The team all cried out, "Go! Mario go!" **/ Prisms: 1a.** cube **b.** rectangular prism **c.** pentagonal prism **d.** triangular prism **2.** 8 vertices, 6 faces, 12 edges **/ Addition: 1a.** 7 581 **b.** 6 678 **c.** 7 684 **d.** 7 795 **2.** 2 346 + 1 439 = 3 785 km |
| **Unit 27** | **Understanding: a.** To show people enjoying themselves on the beach **b.** summer **c.** running on the sand, lying on the beach **d.** Summer holidays are coming. Having a good time at the beach. Enjoying the beach. Or Parent **/ Interpreting: a.** Because they are having fun **b.** Swim between the flags **c.** Remember to keep the rules at the beach **d.** parent **/ Language: a.** near the water **b.** under the umbrella **c.** down the sand **d.** beneath the trees **/ Spelling:** Parent **/ Word Building: a.** aquatic **b.** aqualung **c.** aquarium **d.** aquamarine **e.** aquaplane **/ Sentences:** match **a - h, b - i, c - j, d - f, e - g / 3D Cross-Sections:** △○⬡⬠ **/ Fractions: 1a.**= **b.**< **c.**< d.> **e.**= **f.** > **2a.** colour 2 parts **b.** colour 8 parts **3.** 1/10, 2/10, 3/10, 4/10, 5/10, 6/10, 7/10, 8/10, 9/10 |
| **Unit 28** | **Understanding: a.** true **b.** true **c.** true **d.** true **e.** false **/ Interpreting: a.** being moved or shipped **b.** place of arrival **c.** trees or wood **d.** small, trivial **e.** worked hard **f.** beach, coast **/ Language: a.** who b. whom **c.** which d. whose e. that, which **/ Spelling:** Parent **/ Word Building:** Parent / check jumbled words - spread, manage **Sentences: a.** simple **b.** compound **c.** compound **d.** compound **e.** simple **/ Subtraction: 1a.** 3 515 **b.** 5 144 **2a.** 43, 48, 52, 20, 3, 46, 14, 35 **2b.** 32, 52, 50, 46, 61, 44, 37, 75 **/ Mass: 1a.** 38 kg **b.** 23 kg **2a.** 18 kg |
| **Unit 29** | **Understanding: a.**fresh fruit and water OR cheese and crackers and yoghurt **b.**\$ 6.50 **c.**salad sandwich and egg and lettuce sandwich **d.**water **e.**\$ 3.50 **/ Interpreting: a.** to keep us from getting sick and to help us grow. **b.** 4 **c.** yoghurt milk cheese **d.** fresh fruit and water **e.** bread rolls, sandwiches, bread, crackers |
| **Unit 30** | **Revision: 1a.** adjective, adverb **b.** adjective, adjective **c.** adjective, adverb **2a.** these **b.** this **c.** that **d.** that **3a.** she was… her mother … **b.** My grandmother… so she… until she… **c.** twenty boys… five girls… a female teacher **4a.** Mr and Mrs Shoesmith were able to find Doctor Fren for Jon⊙ **b.** When The Lion King was showing in Sydney I couldn't wait to go to see it⊙ **c.** The Parliament of Australia is in Canberra⊙ **/ Multiplication: 1a.** 5 x 3 = 15 **b.** 3 x 3 = 9 **2a.** 16 b.18 **c.**35 **d.**20 **e.**14 **f.**40 **g.**18 **h.**24 **/ Multiples and Factors: 1.** Circle: 1,3,5,7,11,13,17 **2.** Colour: 6,12,68,18,32,54, |